Possessions, Ghosts and Guardian Angels

Erica Gammon

RAVEN CREST

BOOKS

Publishing the best in new literary voices

www.ravencrestbooks.com
www.ravencrestbooks.co.uk

Enjoy!

Best wishes

Erica x

INTRODUCTION

Well, hello again Reader and thank you for purchasing this book and for deciding that you might like a few shivers into the bargain.

This is my third True Paranormal stories anthology and, as previously, all of them have been given to me by the wonderful people who use social media. I couldn't have done this without them, so a big THANK YOU goes out to all of the people who contributed. There is also a very well-known name in the paranormal field hidden away in this one! I have got some previous contributors to come in too; again – thank you all.

I felt the time was right to gather as many true stories as I could for you to enjoy. Some are not too ghostly, some are just disturbing. Lots of them are just creepy! (Make sure all your doors are locked before you settle down to read.)

I hope you enjoy this book that so many helped me to put together. Without those intrepid souls who make the effort to go and look for these spirits, entities and whatever may lurk out there in the dark, you would never be reading about them. Some people find them without even having to look.

I have given them here for you exactly as they were given to me with no changes (except spelling maybe!).

Please feel free to leave a review about what you have read, be it this book or my others. It may be good, bad or indifferent, but they all help us to become better at what we do and makes your experience of what we write more of what you enjoy (or not, as the case may be!).

So, cuddle up on the sofa or snuggle down in bed … we're off on our journey into the scary lands beyond!

THE STORIES

This story is from Aaron Collins. He is the co-founder of NW Paranormal and is from Gresham, Oregon. He is also a contact from the wonderful world that is social media.

My first paranormal experience terrified and excited me all at once. I was ten years old and I was spending the night with a friend who lived two doors down from us. His home had the same interior layout as my house.

I awoke in the middle of the night to use the rest room; the house was so dark I had to feel my way to the bathroom. When I was done in the bathroom, I had my left hand on the light switch and the other on the door knob. I opened the door and, just as I was about to turn the light off, I saw a woman dressed in a long black robe with long black hair and no face! I mean, there was skin pulled over her skull, but there was no definition of her eyes or her mouth. The only recognizable feature was the nose. I was absolutely terrified! In that split second I turned the light off and ran into the dark, bumping into the walls as I ran to my friend's room. Just as I entered my friend's room I leaped into the air and landed on my friend's bed in sheer terror!

As I landed on the bed, my friend's Chihuahua, who had managed to make himself comfortable while I was in the bathroom, yelped as I landed on him. Needless to say, I had to go back to the bathroom before long. I had to know what I had seen.

That was the beginning of my quest for the paranormal. Some people have asked over the years if it could possibly have been my friend's mum. No – she had short hair and a face! I know what I saw, as the image has been burned into my memory since 1979.

This is a story from a lady in Australia who I have been in contact with via Facebook. She wishes to remain anonymous and I shall respect her wishes.

For as long as I can remember, we've shared our house with unseen tenants – possibly previous owners, renters, or friends and family. My mother first moved into the place in 1974, and from that moment unusual things started happening. A bottle of nail polish set down on the hearth vanished, reappearing behind the couch. Items disappearing and then popping up in unexpected places – or, as in several cases through the years, appearing front and centre of a shelf, drawer, cupboard etc. after it had been checked multiple times.

My oldest sister, a high school student in the late '70s, had a friend over and was telling her about some of the odd happenings in the house. The friend – whose name I forget (this happened before my time) – scoffed and stated that, "Ghosts don't exist". Within moments she'd gone white and was staring up toward the ceiling. A teapot, on the topmost shelf, was slowly spinning in a circle. The friend never came over again.

Other items of various shapes and sizes have completely vanished; in one notable case, again in the late '70s, another of my sisters threw something across the laundry room – and it disappeared in mid-air. Forty years later, it still remains lost.

Voices calling our names; strong scents throughout the house; cold spots – all of them have been experienced by each of us. Many times, through the years, I've been home alone, when I've heard the front door open, slam shut, and heard voices. I've had conversations with the new arrivals – who I've thought were my mother and sister – but when I've entered the room the voices came from, it was empty. We've all heard our names being called when home alone, and seen figures in our peripheral vision. A friend of the family who died of AIDS more than twenty years ago has returned for visits, as has another friend who died suddenly. An appearance my mother had from her own mother, who died in 1963 in England, warned her of an accident one of my nieces and I were to experience the next day.

Never have we felt frightened, or sensed any violence from our unseen friends. They are pranksters, often giving us cause for amusement as well as frustration. We don't know how many spirits are here, but they seem to watch over us, apparently with affection (one night my mother checked on my younger sister only to find a figure leaning over my sister's sleeping form, stroking her arm).

Figures walking past windows; reflections in the mirror; sudden depressions in empty chairs; for a brief time, my mum, younger sister and myself kept seeing a short form scurrying about (obviously not a cat or dog – we only had three small birds in cages) and it gave each of us a sense of discomfort.

One night, about three in the morning, there was an almighty crash in the lounge room and a female voice screamed, 'GET OUT OF MY HOUSE!' My mother and I raced out of our bedrooms at the same time and shot into the lounge room only to find – nothing. Nothing had fallen; nothing was broken. We figured that one of our 'housemates' had taken it upon themselves to evict the horrid little creature that had suddenly appeared, because after that night it was never seen or felt again.

Apart from that brief time, we've never had need to be afraid of our friends ... though I did seem to anger them when I was a teenager. Unsure of how many spirits we shared the house with, I joked one day that it would be interesting to have a medium come to our house and introduce us to everyone, so we could learn names and history. After a few murmurs of interest and general comment, the topic was forgotten. The next morning, when I was dressing, I saw something reflected in the mirror. Violent red claw marks raked from my shoulders down my back; four angry lines on each side. Not believing my eyes, I called my mum and sister to verify my discovery, which they did, both amazed and horrified. There was no pain, but the marks were harsh and long.

I'd remembered my jokey comment of the day before, regarding the possibility of bringing a medium into the house, and apologised profusely for upsetting 'them'. I promised I had only been fooling, and that I would never make any sort of frivolous comment again. Within twenty minutes, the marks were completely gone.

I know there are many people who don't believe in spirits and the afterlife – my partner is one of them – but I think having been raised in such an active environment, it would have been hard to remain indifferent and unbelieving.

This is a story I had from a previous contributor Brian Holloway, previously a co-host on The Ghost Trail, a paranormal show aired in Gibraltar. He has since moved to the UK and decided that he would like to give another story for this book, as he has had some very peculiar experiences with a Ghost Hunting App he and a friend have developed ... not in a good way either. The App has not been taken out of circulation and is still being developed further. It proves you have to be very careful with dealing with the paranormal, in whatever way you interact with them; Brian also live streams on YouTube on Wednesday nights if you want to see for yourself what he does. This is his story, in his own words.

Since leaving the TV show and moving to the UK, I got into developing Apps for use in the paranormal research field. One of them seems to be too successful. When people used it, they got some really weird shit happening to them; some things were so bad that they ended up in hospital!

One professional team used the App during one of their investigations. I warned them to be very careful when they used it; it was very powerful, it seemed to me. As they started to use the App the whole atmosphere of the place changed: it had been normal before, but now it was feeling a whole lot different. The voices they got coming through the App were very dark, even menacing, in their tone and what they were saying. The atmosphere became oppressive. It became a dark and creepy place.

As one voice came through, one of the members of the team turned and saw something. He hadn't any idea of what it could have been. More voices came through with messages like, "die you." At this point some people left, not willing to go any further in what they felt was turning into a very threatening situation.

When I got to hear about this, I decided it really was time I gave it a more thorough test myself. So, on one of my live streams I did; I decided to run it with a friend of mine, J. He ran what I came to call the "naughty" one, while at the same time I ran one which was safer. Within minutes the App (the bad one) started getting messages through it. J could tell something was very wrong. He really started panicking, and needed a moment to calm himself down. I then asked the question to the App I was using, "What is happening to J?" Straight away the answer came back, "It's there." This is verifiable as it is shown on the YouTube channel. At one point a message came through, "It's going to hurt him." I became really worried about J then, as he was still in a state of panic. J went into a room next door and posted a photo of himself. He had removed his shirt and clearly showing on the picture is a bruise on his back the size of a baseball! It was in such a position that he could no way have managed to do this himself. He swore it wasn't there before.

Anyway, this interaction went on for about another hour; everything I got coming through was exactly corroborated as J got the same things I did. I came to the conclusion that the App we had developed worked perfectly well and as it was meant to, with the exception that everyone who used it got hurt or had bad things happen to them in some way. Every time the App was used, everything went bad … very quickly!

After I had really tested the App, I started to experience some weird crap myself. One night I was in the bedroom and my wife told me to look at the mirror on the wardrobe. It had concertina-type mirrors which made up the doors. As I looked, I saw that there were two massive handprints showing on one of them, at least twice the size of a man's hand. Apart from that in itself being unusual, the prints seemed to only have three fingers! I was really shocked as it also seemed to me that whatever had made the imprints had to have been inside the wardrobe in the first place. They were in such a position that the mirror would have to have been at an angle, the prints looking like they had been made by something trying to pull itself out! I photographed the prints and tried to re-create them. This is why I know how it must have been accomplished. This, by the way, has relevance to what would happen later.

A few days later, I was using one of the Apps and watching a live stream with a friend of mine. I showed her the picture I had taken of the hand prints and asked, "what was that?" The App came back with the answer, "David."

It is at this point that I should tell you that this "David" is something that appeared for the first time on one of the Ghost Trail shows, on an investigation we were doing. It has shown itself in some way on every investigation I have done since. It is a very negative and menacing presence and seems to have decided it is me he wants to be with.

Anyway, the friend I was watching the live stream with started to get very interested in "David". I said to her, "Don't go there. He is not someone you can trust. He has come through on every stream we have done. He's really not a nice person."

People who watched the live streams also got interested in "David" and started asking questions about him too.

The friend I was watching with that night asked loads of questions about him. I warned her again not to. She said, "It's OK, I have had some weird stuff happen to me, it will be all right." Again, I told her not to go there; "It's not good at all." I knew from past experience with him that if you started to call him out or disrespect him in any way, things would go very bad, very quick.

She telephoned me a few days later and I asked, "What's up?" She told me that she had gone home and had asked out loud about "David", then she started to criticize and wind him up. It seems all the time she was doing this, it was very quiet. Suddenly the was a terrific BANG right next to her, almost as if someone had let a firework off. Needless to say, she jumped a mile high.

The next day got even worse for her. She lives in a flat with two big burly ex-army guys above, and a single guy on the floor below her. She was doing stuff in her flat when she said that the atmosphere in her flat suddenly changed, for no reason. She said she instantly knew something was very wrong.

From upstairs there came the sound of a man screaming. She ran up to their flat in a panic to see what had happened. One of the guys was shaking from head to foot and the other one was in a similar state. She asked them what was happening and the one shaking badly told her, "We were watching TV when, all of a sudden, there was a weird feeling in the room; it wasn't anything to do with what we were watching. Then we saw a really big shadow cross the wall and it stopped right by the TV. It must have been seven feet tall! But what I remember most was that the hands only had three fingers." You must bear in mind these guys knew nothing about my experience, nor had they been watching the live stream.

When she told me about this I was stunned to find that someone with no knowledge of what had been going on had actually had this experience. My actual thoughts were, "Holy shit!"

A little while after this happened, my friend had a blackout and it scared her enough that she went into hospital to make sure there was no medical reason for it. They couldn't find any reason for it and she said that, just before it had happened, she felt a really strange sensation come over her. That was all she could recall.

She got back to her flat and she met the guy who lived below her and he asked how she was feeling now? Then he told her what had happened to him.

He said that had been sitting doing various bit and pieces, but the next he remembers is standing in the bathroom, with no knowledge of going there. The worst thing was he was standing in the middle of smashed bathroom mirror and bits of the wood it was mounted on, in splinters all around him. He didn't believe in the paranormal, but did have to admit it was a bloody strange thing to have happened.

Another woman I was working with wanted to try the "naughty" App out herself. I thought to myself, "Oh no, not again!" I told her, just like the woman before, "Don't go there! I don't think it's safe! You could really end up hurt!" But she said, "I'm a tough girl and I've dealt with really weird stuff before." I told her "David" would probably come through on it and if he did, don't mock him, or wind him up in any way. I told her to always treat him with respect. I told her if she didn't, she was in for a really bad day.

Now, I can't stop people using this App, but I did tell her it was really fucked up. But she insisted it would be all right. So she used it. She came to regret that decision pretty quickly, as what happened to her is the most severe thing so far.

Afterwards, she told me as soon as she turned the App on a voice came through. (What I found strange was that it didn't hurt her then). She talked to it and it was "David". She didn't just talk to him; she mocked him, too. A bad mistake!

The next morning she tried to get out of bed, but found her back was very sore and her ribs hurt too. In fact, the pains were getting worse and worse. She went downstairs as her Mum lived there. She asked her Mum to look at her back to see if she could see the reason it was hurting so much. When she turned to look at her Mum, she had turned white with shock. She told her that the whole of one side of her back was black – not black and blue like a bruise; just black! There was also a hand print on her back on the side there was no bruising. The pain was getting worse by the minute. She went to the hospital who obviously wanted to know how she got into that state. She told them she had been attacked by someone. They would never have believed her otherwise.

The staff found that, apart from the bruising, she had two cracked ribs and severe internal bruising too; she had been attacked with such force. I believe it was "David" who had done this to her. I did warn her, but never would have imagined that something so bad could, or even would, have happened to her.

It got to be so bad, even to the point on every live stream I did "David" would come in and make his presence known. He seems to be able to take over, and a really weird one was when I was walking around with my SLS camera in my own flat and I saw a figure floating above my dining room table. It was just hanging there. So, I asked it, "Who are you?" Immediately the reply I got back was "David". So, I said, "Hello David." I thought that this was my opportunity, finally, to find out who or what he was, what he wanted and why was he affecting people so badly and viciously, so I started asking him questions, "Why are you doing these things?"

David said, "Because I can."

At this point the camera also picked up three figures sitting at the table. I thought, "What the hell is this?" So, I asked them what they were doing here. I got the answer that they were trying to leave through a portal, but

"David" was guarding it and not letting them through. You could see on the camera that they were actually sitting on the seats at the table. One of them was a smaller figure than the two others. I asked them, "Why can't you leave?" the answer was, "He won't let us." I then asked "David" why he was keeping them here and not letting them through. The answer to that was, "Because I am the Gate Keeper." I asked "David", "Did you create this doorway in and out? You don't have the right to keep these people here; they don't want to be here." I told the figures to go and that he had no control over them. Having said that, two of the larger figures tried to climb onto the table and actually went. The smaller figure was still sitting at the table. It was a female and she said, "I can't leave. He is stopping me." So, I asked "David", why he was keeping her here?

He said, "She's mine."

I couldn't really believe all that was going on. It was like having a conversation with a real person, all the time the SLS camera was capturing it all. I found out from "David" that my house has more than one portal. There is one in/near the TV, the shadow people run at it and disappear or emerge out of it when it is turned off. There is also another in the bedroom. So, I went in with the SLS camera to see.

I saw a figure standing there; when it became aware of me it froze, then ran full force towards the TV in the room and disappeared. I thought, "You have got to be shitting me!" I asked "David" just how many were coming through in a day. Unbelievably, his answer was, "Seventy." I said, "Crap! If you do any damage to my TV, there will be shit to pay!" Shortly after, the TV never worked again; I just couldn't get it to turn on.

Even though "David" is capable of being very dangerous, in no way is he a demon, even though he guarded the portal so no one could leave, as he has been around for so long and has been so intimidating.

11

I finally got to find out what he is. He is worse than a demon.

But, before I go into what he actually is, I must tell you about the next night after I made the TV joke. "David" came again. This time he brought another figure with him; it was a very weird-looking one. So, I asked, "Who is that figure with you?" and, as plain as day, "David" said, "The Devil." I said, "So, to mess with us again, you've bought the Devil?" He said, "Yes." Well, by this time the atmosphere in the room was so thick you could have cut it with a knife.

"David" said to me, "There is something wrong." I said, "You're not shitting me there is!" I thought: is he playing with us, or has he really gone and done something that stupid? Because that is what he does repeatedly; he thinks he is the boss; that he is in charge and not me.

All of a sudden a voice came through the box I was using. It was a lovely voice and it said, "You need help." I thought I had enough trouble here already. So, I asked, "Who are you?" It answered by the name of George. Who the heck was he? Everyone on the live stream heard it say, "I am an Angel." Of course, my usual reply was, "You've got to be shitting me!" I looked at the camera and said, "People are going to think we are insane!" I didn't know what to do. If it wasn't for the fact that everything that was going on was being caught by the camera, people would think I was mad. Everyone could hear that the voice was totally different from the ones we had coming through before. I said, "Right, George, if you could help us that would be brilliant. So what are you going to do? Are you going to take it away?" As soon as I had said it, the devil figure disappeared from the camera! The atmosphere instantly went from thick and oppressive to calmer and normal.

For what felt like the longest time, I didn't know what to say or do. Then I said to the camera, "I don't know what just happened. Was that really devils, demons and angels? What was that?" There were things going on around me, like things moving on their own. What the hell was happening here?

It was exactly at that point I made up my mind that I'd had enough of "David". I needed to know exactly what he was and what I was up against. I should say that we don't just do live streaming; we also use the Ouija board but use that in a more private way. I will say now that we have never had anyone or anything negative happen while we use it; we often connect with family members, but when that happens then it is done totally privately, never on camera. In this instance I asked out and my Dad came through to me. I asked if he knew "David" and the answer was, "Yes." I asked, "What does he look like?" I must say here that I had a theory of what or who he is, but the answer I got back was, "You."

At other Ouija sessions I asked the same questions again, to make sure he was what I was being told. Every time the same answer, "You." It seemed everyone who came through on the board said the same thing; "David" looked like me.

One day on a board session I said outright, "David, I know you are there; you are always there. Who are you?" Over the App which was running at the time, a very matter-of-fact and clear voice came over, "I am you."

It emerged that he was in fact a manifestation of me. He had previously manifested as poltergeist activity and various other negative ways of making sure people knew he was there.

You see, when I was very young I had a pretty crappy life, and a lot of this involved my dad. It seems that all of the stress and anger I felt, I had built up, time and time again, and never released it. But one day, every negative emotion I had ever felt, for some reason (maybe almost like a nervous breakdown?) was the first time "David" made his first presence felt.

I was working on a series called the Ghost Trail in

Gibraltar at the time, but at that precise moment was when all the negativity trapped inside me, for all those years, found its release. It gave itself a name – "David" – and he has actually become a totally separate me! Even though he is attached to me, he thinks for himself and has a separate personality; totally different from me. He does his own thing and I have no control over him at all. When he is not around he goes back inside me; I have no knowledge of him there, or what he does.

It seems that everyone who became close to me got hurt in some form or other. Somehow "David" perceives them as a threat and seems to think that, by doing what he does, he is protecting me in some weird and distorted way. He is so strong; the power this thing has scares me. As I have said, I have no control over him or his actions whatever. He is potentially dangerous, very dangerous. Truthfully, I don't know what to do about it.

Authors note: Brian still live streams on YouTube every Wednesday night. The show is live, and, by the way, he is still making the "naughty" App!

This is a contribution from Chuck Collins, again it was sent in via a request I put on social media.

It was only a few months after we moved in to our house that I realized something was not usual there. I started noticing things being not where I had left them. I found pictures that I had been looking at were being moved around or turned around backwards. I figured it was my kids at first or maybe my girlfriend; then I realized when these things happened we were not home or it was after everyone was in bed.

I questioned them about some of it and no one owned up to it. I then just let it go, until a few weeks later that I discovered that the ceiling fan was on in the living room, but I did not hear the motor running, and that's when I looked over at the switch and noticed it was not even in the on position. I began to really get nervous at this point, because a few pictures moved or turned around could have been done by anyone and maybe they just forgot about it; however a fan working was a totally different thing. I had thought maybe there could be a short in the wiring, but that could not explain the motor not working the fan's movement.

If that was not enough to get me thinking, I was in the basement doing some laundry and I heard small footsteps above me on the living level of the house, and really disregarded them until I realized that no one was home but me; so I went up to check and when I got to that level the footsteps went to the next level, which was the attic. I continued to follow the steps until they stopped at the small room at the back of the attic. I could hear a small child crying in the corner of that room, but I did not see anything.

As I was coming back down the attic stairs, I was hit with an overwhelming sense of coldness and I felt someone or something glide past me, as if they were in a hurry to get out. I was totally frozen and I could not move. I did not really feel scared at first, until I tried to move and nothing gave; then I began to panic and, of course, that is the worst thing to do. After about two or three minutes I just told myself to relax and, once I did, my mobility returned and I just slowly walked out and down the stairs. I thought it was over at that time, but as soon as I turned to go back down the stairs I passed out, and came back only after I heard my girlfriend coming up the stairs, she asked me what had happened and instead of telling her the truth, I said I just tripped.

I kept trying to rationalize it all over the next few days, but I couldn't. A few nights later I heard what seemed to me to be a slicing sound coming from the kitchen. I got up and came down the stairs. The noise had stopped, but a kitchen knife was lying on the floor; I just placed it in the sink and I told myself that it must have been laid close to the side and fell off. It did not explain the slicing sound I had heard but, then again, I had to rationalize it.

I told my girlfriend about the knife on the floor and she told me she did not have a knife like that; all of her knives were small because she was scared to use large knives and I told her that I did not even bring any silverware with me from Montana.

It was now that I decided to tell her about what I had seen and heard for the past few months. She told me about some odd things that she had noticed also. I asked her why she never said anything, and her reasons were the same as mine: who would believe it?

We began to look into the house's history and discovered that it was a place where a family of three had lived in the 1960s. The father was a coal mine worker in Pittsburg before the pit had shut down. He could no longer find work and he slowly went crazy and he ended up killing his wife with a butcher's knife in the kitchen and strangled his six-year-old daughter in the small room at the back of the attic, which was where I had heard the footsteps end. He then hung himself with a cord over the side rail from the attic.

The things that had happened were only during the months of March through June; the rest of the year was quiet, until October when my youngest son was making a video for a Halloween presentation. He and his friend were outside filming from the first floor level to the attic. When he aimed the camera up to the attic he noticed a small face looking down at him, and it was pale white. He came in and told me about it and asked me why his older brother was in the attic. I did not say anything, but his brother was not at home at the time. I knew who it was and could not bring myself to tell him until much later.

I never heard anything else until the following March, when to my surprise my youngest son told me he had a new friend upstairs and she would open the door at night into his room from the attic. His room lead right into the attic from the hallway. He never was scared during the time we lived there, and I just assumed he had never heard anything, but I was wrong, and it goes to show how kids are able to take time to understand where parents panic because we do not.

We did move from that house, only to move next door, since it was a duplex and the new family that moved in were there less than a week. I watched more than four families move in and out of that place in less than two months.

We finally moved to Virginia in July of 2008, but I never will forget that house and the family of three that will never leave.

This is a true story that happened over a period of one and a half years. It happened in Greensburg, PA and I now have a better understanding of what after life and death can hold for those taken before their time.

This is from P Jackson, who is a team member of C.O.P.I. I think this is a very intriguing story and has helped me with the naming of this book.

This is a personal experience I had about five or six years ago on my way to work in the city. We lived at the time up near Algonquin Park in Northern Ontario, Canada. I am a firefighter and, working the shifts I work, I had to leave home around 4:30 am to make it to the city in time for my shift.

This particular time I had an older Chrysler Sebring; the headlights on my car were way out of adjustment and in fact I had ordered new ones that I was waiting for. This long stretch of highway is very secluded and I rarely ever saw another vehicle, other than a bread delivery truck that would pass me going in the other direction. There was never any fear of seeing any police along that road as it's away from the populated areas. The road itself is a smooth, long, twisty stretch with numerous banks and bends weaving its way between towering rock cuts through granite. It was not uncommon to see lots of wildlife along the road as well, ranging from racoons and porcupines to deer and moose.

This particular morning I made my coffee, gathered my things and headed to work. As I wound my way through the huge rock cuts and smooth winding road, I came around a bend about halfway along the route.

In the dip in the road ahead, I could make out very dim lights flashing. As I slowed down and approached the car from behind, it was their four way flashers on but they, as I said, were barely visible. The car itself was a late '70s or '80s maroon-coloured Ford LTD (I have not seen one of those on the road for years before this and haven't seen one since). I realized the car was sitting still in the westbound lane. I pulled around into the oncoming lane and stopped with my passenger side close to their driver's side door. I put my window down and looked over at the driver of the other car. It was a single person – a woman – in the driver's seat, wearing glasses, with dark, shoulder-length curly hair. I asked, "Are you OK? Having car trouble?" She turned to look at me, her hands on the steering wheel at the ten and two position, then turned back, looking straight ahead; no expression on her face as she spoke, "I'm not from around here. I don't know the roads and there are two moose right ahead." She never turned to look at me again, her voice didn't change pitch at all; she then said, "Do you wanna go ahead?" I said, "Sure." I slowly pulled ahead of her and back into the westbound lane. I was probably sitting there talking to her for maybe two-three minutes.

As I started moving up around the bend and in between the rock cut, maybe a distance of 150-250 feet, there they were: two large moose trotting in the westbound lane. I slowly pulled behind them. I could hear their hooves clomping along the pavement. I gave the horn a little honk to see if they would move off the road; instead they turned, looking back at me, and kept going. Once we got to the other end of the rock cut, they ran up the hill into the woods and were gone.

I looked up into my rear-view mirror and to my surprise there was NO car behind me! Corner after corner and straightaways, I never saw any lights or the car again; as if it just vanished!

If she was afraid of driving along the road, it makes no sense that she would have gone anywhere; in fact, I'd think the opposite: that she would have been right behind me.

I did not tell anyone about this for a couple of weeks, including my wife. I was trying to make sense of it. I was thinking that, at that time of night, I would have come around that bend in the road at a speed around 80 mph. Most people that hit a moose do not survive it, let alone TWO moose and a solid granite rock wall at that speed. How could I have heard her talking in a normal low voice over two cars running and her not even looking at me, other than a brief second, as if she was checking who I was? And that car ... as I said, I haven't seen one for years leading up to that night and I have not seen one since. I couldn't even say for sure that her car was running!

I told my wife a couple weeks later and said to her, "I have to tell you something and it makes zero sense to me." I explained the encounter to her and she looked at me, shock on her face as she said, "You met your guardian angel."

I have had it explained to me by a team member that she manifested the car herself and that took a lot of energy; that's why the lights where so dim; and she KNEW I would stop to help her and not just drive around and keep going! I am totally convinced that, had she NOT been there at that spot, on that night, at that exact time, I would most likely NOT be here today. I was told after that, there was a reason she did what she did, and that I had another reason to have it happen. Shortly after this, I rescued a woman from a house fire and often wonder if that wasn't the reason?

This is from Dave Elvey, who is a retired police officer from Kent in the UK. He contacted me from Twitter and I think we can say it is probably all right to trust this one happened!

Intruder at the nursing home

This event took place in the late eighties, yet remains vividly etched into my memory as the incident which revitalised my fascination with the paranormal.

I was a response police constable working in Maidstone, the county town of Kent in South East England. I was on night shift, crewed up with another PC who I shall call 'Scotty', owing to the fact that he was Scottish and I like Star Trek. He was a very dour man, did not suffer fools gladly, but had a cynically dry sense of humour.

It was the early hours of the morning; I think around 3.00 am when we received an emergency call to a small residential nursing home in a village called Loose, located just outside of the town. The call had been made by a member of staff, who was reporting intruders on premises. Fortunately, we were literally minutes away. As we raced to the scene, the call dispatcher informed us that there had been loud banging on the exterior windows, as if someone was trying to break through the shutters, then the staff had heard someone actually walking around on an upper floor when they were all downstairs. Before we stated the obvious, it wasn't a resident as they were all elderly bed-bound patients!

So we arrived, adrenalin pumping, not knowing what to expect. The call dispatcher was still on the telephone to the home, usual practice for an intruder call, so we dashed straight in through the already opened main door. It struck me how utterly terrified the female nurse looked as she held the door for us. 'Where are we going?' I asked.

She pointed at a set of stairs in the main reception area, "Up there." Scotty and I drew our truncheons and torches, and up we went. I recall it being quite a narrow staircase, single file only, with a couple of tight turns which prevented you from seeing around the corner.

Upstairs, it was a very simple layout, just the one floor, turn left for one communal ward and right for another, with built in storage cupboards in the middle; basically nowhere for anyone to go, except past us. Fortunately, a dim light partially illuminated the landing which made our lives easier, as we opened up every one of the cupboards to see if our intruder had tucked themselves away. It never ceases to amaze me the lengths some criminals go to in order to escape capture. They have an inhuman ability to squeeze themselves into the tiniest of spaces, rather like plumbers.

Anyway, the cupboards were clear, so now it was time to search the actual wards, where the lights were well and truly off. Scotty and I stood on the landing, peering into the darkness of the rooms, it seemed like every scrap of light had been sucked out. All the other response cars were dealing with other incidents, so it was just us. We agreed in hushed tones to take a ward each, but all I really wanted at that moment was to turn on every light and shout the usual warnings which, in no uncertain terms, urged the offender to give themselves up quietly. But, for the sake of the residents, who were elderly and quite poorly, that wasn't on the cards, so in we ventured.

I think the two things that unsettled me the most were seeing those blanket-covered forms lying still on their beds and the noises that were coming from them. There were unintelligible mutterings, whimpers, soft weeping and even low chuckles. It wasn't their fault of course – my wife often tells me of the inhuman sounds I make in my sleep – but it was just so unnerving.

I searched under and around every bed and even

double-checked that there was only one occupant in each. Yes, some offenders have been known to hide in plain sight. At one point I remember standing up by a bed, having just checked underneath, and glancing at the person lying on it, only to find them staring at me! I was about to open my mouth to whisper an apology but realised that they were actually still asleep, the chest moving up and down in that slow rhythmic manner of slumber.

Again, all clear; no intruders. I crept back out onto the landing and found Scotty was just emerging from his search. First thing he said to me, looking fairly ashen was, "Bloody hell, Dave; that was a wee bit tense." That was about the most unnerved I'd ever seen him...

Having satisfied ourselves that there were no trespassers still on scene, we made our way back downstairs and found the staff room. There we found four absolutely terrified female members of staff. We quickly reassured them that the building was clear, then sent them off to see if anything was missing, while we checked around the outside of the premises. Reassuringly, all the windows and shutters were undamaged and totally secure. So, no evidence of any attempted forced entry and no intruder to be found. I must say that my curiosity was piqued, so we returned to the staff room where the four ladies were all back from their task. They informed us that there was nothing either damaged or missing anywhere in the building. Scotty was never very good at hiding his opinion and it was clear to me that he was running out of patience with the nurses. But, from my perspective, I was seeing four ladies who had clearly been scared witless and it was time to find out why.

We all gathered in the staff room and were made a nice warm brew. They told us that it had been a busy night; one of the residents had sadly passed away earlier in the day and they had the job of sorting out their personal effects in addition to their usual tasks.

Eventually, once things had settled, they all convened

in the staff room for a well-deserved break. They were quite happily chatting away when everyone suddenly jumped out of their skins, as three louds bangs rocked the shutters on the outside of one of two staff room windows.

For a moment, the women were all a bit shocked and disorientated but, before they could do anything, there were three more louds bangs on the next window. Thinking that someone was attempting to break down the shutters, they collectively ran out of the room and into the reception area. No sooner had they done that, than three more loud bangs came from one of the windows out there, immediately followed by bangs on the next window, then the next one. It was as if there was a person standing at each window of the building, taking turns to smash their fists against the shutters as hard as they could. Not getting any comfort from being in the foyer, they decided to retreat back to the staff room; another reason being that's where the only working telephone for night duty staff was located (no cell phones back then). Really shaken now, they entered the staff room half expecting to see remains of glass and wood scattered on the floor. But there was nothing; all was intact, and, for a moment, everything went quiet.

'Bloody kids or drunks,' one of them had surmised. That seemed as good an explanation as any, even though there had never been any issues in the home's history with attracting anti-social behaviour, but what happened next would blast that theory to smithereens.

Located on a wall in the staff room was a large intercom unit which they used to communicate with each other and monitor the wards upstairs. There was a matching unit on the upstairs landing and it was the usual practice of night staff to leave the intercom in the 'on' position in order that they could actually hear what was going on upstairs in the two wards. Apparently, the unit was super sensitive and could pick up any noise from either ward quite clearly. The ladies currently on duty were very adamant that, by now, they could identify which sounds originated from the residents and the building.

So, back in the relatively safe confines of the staff room, the banging seemed to have stopped. They all stood round, on high alert, ready for the next crescendo. But, instead of that, they all heard through the open intercom the sound of heavy footsteps making their way across the upper landing; very clear, distinctive footsteps. Not light, delicate or unsteady steps, but a determined steady tread.

They looked at each other, stunned, clearly all realising simultaneously that there was nobody in the entire building, apart from the four of them, who was remotely capable of walking up and down like that. Without exchanging a word, one of them just dashed to the telephone and rang 999. While the call was being made, the footsteps seemed to be heading from one side of the building to the other; it seemed to them that they then reached the location of the upper intercom, as if it stood at the top of the staircase, just listening and waiting.

Then all went quiet again and stayed quiet, until they heard the noise of our police car, with its not-very-stealth-like diesel engine chugging up the drive literally minutes later.

Scotty and I then spent some considerable time reassuring the ladies that no intruder remained on the premises and there was no physical evidence to suggest that there was one in the first place. It was quite clear that they were still very distraught and did not want us to leave them, judging by the endless cups of tea and the supply of 'posh' biscuits. The conversation then turned as to what actually caused all of this. There were differing lines of thought: two of the nurses were now definitely considering something supernatural. Another dismissed that entirely, based more on her religious beliefs than anything else. One was still too terrified to think anything and would more likely, not be back for another night shift. Scotty simply laughed at the paranormal suggestion and muttered something about mass hysteria, in between devouring their stock of chocolate biscuits. I was taking middle ground, prepared to be open to any solution, as long as there was evidence to back it up.

We stayed as long as we could, but dawn was looming and it was time to depart. As we were getting our gear together, two of the nurses took the opportunity to fetch some items from an under-stairs cupboard back in reception. They had only been gone literally a minute, when we heard piercing screams from outside the staff room. I shot out there and was confronted by two ashen-faced nurses, both physically shaking. "Footsteps," one of them just about managed to say and pointed to the stairs. "Someone's going up there."

I literally felt the adrenaline surge through my body and was instantly alert and pretty bloody angry at the audacity of this unknown person, as I found myself bounding up the stairs in hot pursuit, not knowing or really caring if Scotty was behind me or not.

I expected to turn a corner on the staircase and be confronted by someone or something any second; I surely must have been right on their tail. But ... nothing! I got to the upper floor and there was nobody in sight. There was absolutely no way that anyone could be that quick. Apart from the bed-bound patients I was truly alone, so I did actually jump in the air as I heard, quite clearly, the sound of heavy footsteps moving away from me, heading for one of the wards.

I was rooted to the spot. My career had been based around tangible, solid evidence so, standing there listening to those footsteps, was something pretty alien for me. Exercising the better part of valour, I didn't feel the need to continue the chase. My mouth agape, I simply stayed as still as a statue until the footsteps seemed just to dissolve away. I made my way back downstairs in a bit of a trance and found Scotty was standing at the bottom, baton drawn, giving his best Scottish scowl. He relaxed when he saw me and obviously realised from my demeanour that all was not well. He simply frowned at me, tutted and walked off muttering, "Not you as well? Mass bloody hysteria."

Once again, we provided the requisite reassurance to the staff but, to be honest, I could have done with a bit myself. After a while we left to head back to the police station. En route, our local control room radioed us requesting a result for the call. After a momentary hesitation I simply used the famous four words that any copper will be familiar with, "Area searched; no trace."

Apparently, nothing remotely paranormal had ever happened at the home before and, as far as I'm aware, nothing happened after these events. Whether it was somehow connected to the resident who had recently passed, I couldn't say. Perhaps it was their way of saying goodbye and wanting to go out with a literal bang. I just wish they had been a tiny bit quieter about it!

Dean McFarlane, from a paranormal information site on Facebook, provided these next few stories for you.

A little introduction: my name is Dean and I live in Romford, East London. As I am telling this story, I am twenty-seven years old, but these events occurred when I was fifteen years old.

I used to visit my mum in Rainham, East London most weekends where she had a three-bedroom maisonette. It wasn't the most appealing of places on the outside, although inside was fairly decent, but it's the activity that sparked interest.

Mum used to have friends stay every so often; they would sleep in her bedroom and she would fall asleep on the sofa in the living room in front of the TV. As I've always been a believer in the paranormal, she would often tell me encounters she was having with a few spirits. One was a middle-aged man, dressed in denim overalls, short brown hair, about six feet tall, rather slim. The second regular visitors were two children: one girl; one boy. You would usually see these two together, rarely one without the other. The third one, which haunted and attacked in mum's room was a massive black mass that would pull people out of bed and have them flee in terror.

I never personally encountered the black mass in a physical sense, but emotionally I would sense it: intense anger, bouts of depression, despair, anxiety, the feeling of entrapment as though I was a prisoner in the room and I wasn't able to leave. If I was in a room at night upstairs, the rooms would appear dimly lit and rather oppressive.

I experienced one encounter with the young boy. Mum said she would often see both the boy and girl around me and sensed they sought comfort in me, as if I was a big brother. We were sitting there watching TV – well, more so talking – when I said, "I'm going to get a drink." As I looked to my right into the kitchen, I saw the small boy on his hands and knees, looking at me and smiling from the far end of the kitchen; he was holding a toy car in his right hand. I looked again to assure myself he was there, and he was, so I smiled and he suddenly vanished. He was wearing a red and black striped t-shirt, jeans, and he had short black hair and a round face, as though a bit stocky. Shortly after I got my drink, mum said she saw both the boy and girl sitting in front of my feet watching TV as we sat there talking. I cannot remember the description for the girl as I never saw her.

One particular weekend, during the summer of 2006, I stayed at mum's and shortly after my arrival she rushed me to her bedroom to show her me her makeup mirror. There was a message smeared on the mirror saying, 'Soon'.

We decided to do our own little investigation to try and gain contact with the spirit behind the message to find out its motives. Now, neither myself or my mum belong to any paranormal investigation groups, but we knew how to gain contact.

The Friday night, we decided not to do anything but relax. I was asleep on the living room floor and mum was sitting on the sofa to my right. I suddenly woke up in a tremendous amount of pain, as though it was a severe cramp. The burning was intense. As I looked at mum to tell her what I was experiencing, she looked at my legs, frozen in fear (which takes a lot for us). I asked, "Why are you staring at my legs? They are burning so much." She replied slowly, in a trance-like state, "There's a dog, German Shepherd, chewing at your legs ... there's a man in the doorway, laughing." I asked her to describe him and she said, "Very tall, very dark," which sent a few chills down my spine. Suddenly the pain stopped.

Saturday night came and we decided to do our little investigation to draw the energy out and confront it. We placed the makeup mirror on the dining table, with the message still intact and began an E.V.P session. The first question we asked was, "Who are you?" to which we received a reply abruptly saying, "F**K OFF!" We continued to ask questions and received no answers.

With the room all dark with a few candles lit, I decided to take some pictures on my phone. The first few pictures were normal and nothing showed. Suddenly, I snapped a few shots in the doorway between the living room and hallway, and I caught a white figure peering around the doorway with its arm hanging around the frame, as though this figure was peeking around at us. I snapped a final shot and the picture came out all grainy. Upon looking, I noticed a grainy face with a sinister smile, but when I flipped the picture the other way, it revealed a skull. When I showed mum, it sent chills down her spine as she shouted, "THAT'S THE MAN WHO ATTACKED YOU!"

I took my phone into school the following Monday and showed all my friends and even teachers. Without saying a word, I showed them all and asked them to point out what they saw. They all said the same thing: a sinister face one side, a skull the other. Sadly, I no longer have the pictures and, shortly after, mum moved out as she couldn't cope there any longer.

This story is Dean McFarlane's next offering for you.

This particular one is more of a temporary possession that came from nowhere.

This event took place in the summer of 2011. I was living in Cambridgeshire with my dad, step-mum, three sisters and three brothers at the time. My ex-partner, who I'll call Charlotte, was very sceptical about the paranormal and wasn't a solid believer. We would often have discussions on whether or not ghosts really existed.

My Nan had passed away when my mum was only a baby. She lost her fight to breast cancer as she refused treatment to have my mum. Now, I always sense my Nan when she's around me, and that's quite often.

One particular weekend, Charlotte and I were up quite late watching films and having a cuddle, when we decided to go downstairs and make a cup of coffee. As we stood in the kitchen, preparing the coffee, she suddenly walked off out into the garden in her nightdress. The weather wasn't particularly great so that made it a bit odd. She suddenly came in and stood in the corner of the living room in the dark. All I could see was her long blonde hair and white nightdress. Her face seemed a bit blank, as though there were no features, but that could have been the lack of light. I asked her, "What are you doing?" but received no reply. I turned the light on and I saw her face. Her light blue eyes locked onto mine with no facial expression. I sat her down on the sofa and said, "Talk to me! What's going on with you?!", to which I got a smile. She placed her right hand on my face and said, "I am so proud of you. I can't say the same for your mother and Aunt Theresa," (not her real name). I said, "What do you mean?" and I got, "My daughters don't seem to have family values, and your mum put you through hell, and Theresa has turned her back on all of you. You've always stood by your mum despite everything, and I am so proud of you, you are the grandson I would have always wanted. I love you, and I am always here," and she then kissed me on the cheek. I started to cry; she brushed the tears away and smiled. Next thing, Charlotte said, "What are we doing downstairs?! Why are you crying?! What's going on?" I just looked at her and explained. She had chills, but she said, "Did it bring you comfort?", to which I told her it did. She gave me a kiss and we cuddled and she told me she loved me.

Now, you're probably wondering what makes me think she was possessed. Well, I'll explain. I never really mentioned my mum's side of the family to her, due to various complications, and she wouldn't really ask unless I spoke about them. Not once did I ever mention my aunt's name, but she suddenly knew it. That comfort still sticks with me today but, ever since then, I've only felt her presence and we haven't had a solid interaction like that since.

What also makes this nicer is that I was diagnosed with Borderline Personality Disorder just weeks before the encounter and I was struggling. Always remember: when you're feeling low, loved ones who have passed on are there with you.

Here is Dean's story number three.

When I was seven years old, I lived in a flat in Grays, Essex. We lived on the top floor of a three-story block. My sister and I shared a bedroom as it was only a two-bedroom flat. Our bedroom window was at the back of the block, so our view from the window was of Grays train station, the community garden and a graveyard between the garden and station.

Now, I had a friend in school, who I'll call Lisa, who

wasn't well. She had a rare illness that meant she wouldn't live a very long life. I always looked after her in school and made sure none of the other kids were horrible to her. One particular night I was lying in bed with the lights dimmed; my sister was fast asleep on the bunk below me. I remember having this intense feeling of dread, as though something wasn't right; something was going to happen, but I didn't know what.

As I lay there, staring at the ceiling, I saw what I can only describe as death itself, flying through the wall next to me and hovering above me, laughing. This wasn't exactly your stereotypical reaper. This reaper had a cloak on, but it wasn't black, it was navy blue; he didn't have a scythe, he had my friend Lisa on his back screaming for help. I was frozen in fear; my mind couldn't process what I was seeing.

He dropped her on my lap and flew into my parent's bedroom, as she sat on my lap screaming at me to help her. All I could do was stare and cry in fear. As she faded, I threw my covers off and darted into the living room and threw myself into my mum's arms as she sat there watching a paranormal documentary on TV. Mum asked me to describe what I saw, so I told her. Scared herself, we slept on the sofa that night.

When I returned to school, I had found out that Lisa had sadly passed away and lost her battle to the illness. At first I was sad, but then an intense shot of fear hit me as that image was burned into my mind. To this day, I cannot forget it.

This story is from a group who I saw on Twitter and who were good enough to send this story for you. It goes to prove, you should really be careful in what you do!

East Coast Spirit Chasers St Albans Sanatorium in Radford, VA, submitted by Jennifer Hodge and Nick Waskiw.

In mid-summer of 2017, East Coast Spirit Chasers paranormal team ventured to Saint Albans Sanatorium in Radford, VA to investigate one of the most haunted locations in the United States. Once a boy's school that condoned bullying, then turned into a hospital for the mentally ill, Saint Albans is notorious for its tumultuous spirits. On this particular investigation, we were not disappointed with the amount of evidence and activity that was witnessed by our team members.

We started our investigation in the bowling alley, which is reportedly haunted by two females: the spirit Allie, who is rumoured to be a daughter of one of the patients; and Gina, who was murdered nearby the sanatorium. A dark presence is also reported to oppress the female spirits that have taken up residence in the alley.

Once the team had the multiple pieces of investigation equipment placed out on the lanes of the alley, they started lighting up with activity when we asked questions in relation to the female spirits being guarded by a darker force. Two investigators had experiences of being touched on their shoulder by a soft hand.

Trigger props that are stuffed animals with lighted sensors on them, lit up when specific questions were asked about this particular dark force. Another investigator immediately started acting in a negative manner and had to leave the area.

Towards the end of the time in the bowling alley, a feeling of gloom was affecting many of the investigators and one felt a hand start to choke her neck. At the same time the investigator felt her neck being choked, another team member started to well up with tears. It was decided at this point that all team members should leave the bowling area as something dark was starting to loom over the investigation.

After that we moved on to what is known as the suicide bathrooms. As many as four suicides are known to have taken place in this area. During our time spent investigating that area, we came in contact with a female spirit who reportedly secretly kept her baby in a jar in one of the closets of the rooms, and in her grief committed suicide because the jar was found by staff.

In order to try to make contact with her, an investigator brought in a baby doll that cries when a spirit intercepts the electromagnetic field, signalling the presence of something not seen.

We placed the baby doll in the same closet where she was rumoured to have put her baby, and the doll started making the crying noises, indicating that a spirit was interacting with it. It was at this time that a team member had their shirt pulled in a downward motion, and other team members witnessed it being pulled by an unseen force. We decided to see if we moved the doll out of the closet if the female would still interact, and she did. A pervasive feeling of sadness took over the room.

We then endeavoured to explore some unknown areas of the sanatorium and had great interaction in every room that we went in. Because of the size of the sanatorium, the team could have spent the entire weekend there and still not explored all of the areas.

Toward the end of the investigation, several members felt the location to have a very ominous hold over them and decided to stop investigating a bit early. A few members decided to go into the boiler room, which many who had investigated the location previously have warned has the darkest presence affecting females.

Once in the boiler room, the four investigators who were still holding strong to finish out the night, decided to hold a portal session so that they could communicate verbally with the presence. While trying to communicate with this presence, a female investigator felt her shirt being pulled and suddenly felt extremely dizzy. It was at this point that pig squealing noises started coming through the portal and an investigator who was knowledgeable in demonology advised that could indicate a demonic force.

It was at this time that the last members still investigating decided to call it a night, in fear that something unsavoury was trying to overtake the investigation.

After our experiences at this location, we are more aware of the darker presences that fill the spirit world and have adapted our investigations to include a heavy focus on spiritual protection. Still very curious, we will venture back to the sanatorium to hopefully make further contact and figure out why these presences linger, while keeping a more guarded approach when making contact with unknown entities.

Hi, my name's Julie and I own Feather Foot Paranormal. As this happened over a decade ago I haven't written it word for word and have added a couple of things including my conclusion. The story isn't long, so I hope it's OK. It happened in Sydney, Australia.

I called it Ghost Family

Myself and my boyfriend moved into a fairly large single-storey house in Sydney's North Shore with a number of our friends. When we first moved in, it was evening, and when I walked in with one of my friends, we got to the very long and dark hallway and just stopped frozen as we were both feeling freaked out; it was really weird.

We didn't know what we were in for.

I have always been fascinated with the paranormal so normally this would be right up my alley, but I am also a bit of a sensitive; I am in tune with different energies. Something didn't feel right with the house; nothing demonic or similar, just creepy.

It started affecting me in a way that I started getting anxiety about going to bed. Sometimes I would feel more comfortable sleeping in the lounge room with the light on; this was before any of us experienced anything.

Then a few of my housemates, as well as myself, started to have bad dreams, even some other friends who would stay for a couple of nights.

Then my most prolific experience happened one night. I was sleeping in my bed and woke suddenly right on 3am. I was lying awake and it could have been five minutes later coming from somewhere in the middle of my room (it was a decent-sized room) I heard a little child's voice call 'Mum', like any child when they are calling for their mother or looking for them; it kind of drags out a little so it was like 'Muuuuuum'. I sat up, so startled and turned to my boyfriend and cried, "Did you hear that?" He said he hadn't, although years later he admitted he had heard something. The thing is, only adults lived in this house; there were no children. I couldn't sleep without a light on after that.

Some of my housemates said they had seen either an older woman or a little girl, with hair in plaited pigtails. I never saw any apparitions myself, but I heard and felt things; the hallway and one of the bathrooms creeped me out so that I couldn't even bring myself to shower alone, which I know was silly, but I just couldn't.

I felt it was more the house itself that affected me than the spirits themselves, as I felt there was more to it than just being haunted; the house feeling full of dread was what made me feel sick and anxious.

While I was living there, the spirits who resided there were a middle-aged lady and about four or five children. My boyfriend found that out when he consulted a medium. The lady spirit told the medium she was sorry if it was them making me sick and that they would leave. They did, because when I got home I could feel their absence, although the house still made me uncomfortable. I found out why six years later from my boyfriend; turns out this house was once used as a funeral home. I guess all the dead that passed through this place left residual imprints which I was picking up. I didn't know I was gifted as an Empath and had some of the 'Clair' abilities at the time, so I didn't know how to handle it.

My boyfriend is now my husband; this happened possibly thirteen years ago. I got into paranormal investigation about nine years ago when I moved to Queensland and I have run my own team for about three years, which my husband is a part of. Now that I know more about my abilities and learning how to use them, I am no longer scared or anxious about any experiences I have, and I have learnt so much more about the paranormal.

Gavin Canavan was born in Co. Wicklow in 1979. He became interested in demonology at an early age. He was just fourteen when he saw what he thought was a spirit. Gavin has been practicing religious demonology for the last ten years. He has built up his knowledge in his chosen field by continuous study and experience. He has delved into other areas of the paranormal world such as mediumship, dowsing, paranormal investigation, parapsychology and distance healing. He took on all of these fields of study to educate himself in what works and what does not. (GAVIN ONLY WORKS WITH RELIGION TO CLEAR HOMES AND CLIENTS). He works closely with some of America's leading demonologists. Gavin's work has taken him on amazing journeys of discovering what is really out there. He continues to help families in need across Ireland and further afield. If Gavin cannot help you he will not rest until he finds someone who can. Jessie joined the team in 2016 and is case manager. They can be contacted on gavdemonologist@yahoo.com. All cases are confidential and are free of charge. This family has given permission to tell their story and their names have been changed to protect their identities.

In January 2017 the team were contacted by Joseph. The previous November 2016, Joseph and his sister Helen had taken part in a public paranormal investigation. This is when the public attend an investigation with a paranormal team in a haunted location. Joseph explained that he and his sister had not really believed in the paranormal world but just wanted to try something different. They wanted to be entertained and felt that this was something new and interesting. They enjoyed it so much they went to the same haunted location with the same paranormal team on three occasions. On the third night, Joseph entered a room of the old house by himself. Encouraged by the paranormal team, Joseph took part in a mirror scrying experiment. As he sat alone in the pitch-black room, little did Joseph know his world was about to change.

Joseph and his sister Helen had been grounded by the paranormal team before and after the investigation. Grounding is asking for protection from whatever you believe in. For example, if you believe in angels you ask them to surround you with love and light to keep you safe. People also imagine roots coming from their feet going into the ground and asking for a ball of white light to surround them like a shield to keep them safe. Every paranormal team has their own way of grounding people. This dark entity had little regard for the paranormal team's feeble attempt to protect the public on this occasion.

At the end of the day you are willingly giving up your free will once you have entered a location where suspected paranormal activity may be. Helen and Joseph had gone for fun to see if it was all real. Were there spirits out there? Little did Joseph know, but an entity had attached to him that night and his life was about to take a turn for the worse. Their curiosity in the world unknown has now become their reality.

On the 9th January 2017, Joseph contacted Gavin. He told his story of what had happened. He was very truthful in his account, which is most important when dealing with cases. Without all the facts, it can be difficult to determine what the best way to proceed with the case is. He explained about the paranormal investigation and that he had taken part in mirror scrying. He went on to explain the sinister happenings within his home which were affecting both Joseph and his sister Helen.

He had contacted a lady, looking for help, prior to contacting Gavin. This lady had visited his home. She told him that something had attached to his soul and it was attempting to pull his soul away from his body. She advised Joseph to ground himself every morning and send light into each room of the house every day. She blessed the home and the family. Joseph followed this advice but it did nothing to help his situation. Joseph was eventually led to Gavin and so their journey began. In his own words, Joseph describes exactly what was happening in his home.

"It all started seven weeks ago, touches my whole body head to your toes, knocking sounds in the bedroom and sitting room at all times, gets worse when in bed and relaxed states, heart beats fast, stomach growls, feeling very warm and sweaty, bad smell in room, birds singing and making noise in the middle of the night; birds don't sing at night. It's starting to growl at Helen and makes noises in her room. It makes us feel dizzy as if something is going in and out of our body and it takes our breath away. We have seen big black orbs floating past us, weird dreams, and black shadows."

Within one of his dreams, Joseph describes being in a building. He recognizes it as the old house that he went investigating in. He is back where all this started; the night of the paranormal investigation.

He could see silhouettes of people standing around in a room. Suddenly a dark figure starts to swirl around him. It keeps asking Joseph to let it in but Joseph refuses and asks it to go away. The figure begins mocking Joseph, by laughing at him. When Joseph woke, he felt strange and knew something was seriously wrong. He describes a second dream where he could see a black shadow figure on the top floor of this haunted building. It moved across from one window to another room. Joseph noticed it has now changed into a black hooded figure. It comes straight up to Joseph's face and startles Joseph so much, he wakes.

Gavin immediately recognizes all of this information as

the infestation stage of the entities process. This dark entity was trying to build fear within the family and it was succeeding. It was looking for the invitation from Joseph to open doors to unleash its true power. A home visit was required.

Upon meeting Joseph and Helen, they presented themselves as very nice and welcoming people. They are down to earth and very pleasant. The family were first asked to give an interview. They were clear with their information and were willing to participate in answering questions. Although they appeared very shy at first, they were good communicators and did not hold back. There is no history of mental illness within the family. They are not on drugs and do not suffer from alcohol dependency. Their home is a three-bedroom bungalow in the middle of the country and is homely.

There is no evidence of occult objects in the home, instead there is evidence of religious icons and pictures scattered around the walls of the home.

EMF readings were normal and there are no issues with carbon monoxide within the home. From talking to the family, it was clear they had no idea of the dangers of the paranormal or they would never have taken part in the paranormal investigation; they would have stayed away. On this visit Gavin walked around the property and clearly sensed some dark energy. After sensing this energy, Gavin decided on the best approach. Every case is different and may need different levels of intervention.

Using his years of experience, Gavin proceeded in what he thought was best. Both Helen and Joseph were given religious healing. Gavin challenged the entity with religious provocation. This can be dangerous if you do not have experience in such matters. It takes much preparation to get to this level, and if you do not know what you are doing you can put yourself and the family in more danger and make the situation worse. The entity did not show itself on this occasion. A deliverance was performed anyway. Gavin advised Joseph and Helen to get a priest into the house to say a mass. As Gavin and Jessie left the home, they knew it would not be the last they heard of Joseph and Helen, as whatever was attached to Joseph was strong. It can take months and months to fully clear a house or to remove an attachment this strong.

As expected, it was not long before Joseph was back in contact again. He explained how he had contacted a priest who came and blessed the house, but would not perform a mass in the home. Joseph contacted a second priest and he did come and perform a mass in the home for the family.

Joseph reported that there was still activity going on, but not as strong. Gavin told Joseph to continue with the advice he had previously given him and to get back in contact if the activity did not stop. He also advised to keep a journal of events.

Gavin believed at this stage that this case may need to go further. Part of being a good demonologist is in knowing your limitations. Failure to see when more interventions are needed may have detrimental effects. You are dealing with people's lives and therefore it cannot be a case of ego and pride getting in the way.

At this time, Gavin was working another case also. This case involved a young woman who had used a Ouija board. She also did not think there was any harm in what she was doing, until her life was turned upside down. Gavin had removed the Ouija board. He brought it into his home and blessed it. When Gavin has cases where objects are the trigger, he always removed them for the families' protection, but this board appeared to kick start a series of events in Gavin's own life.

Now it appeared that Gavin was the one who needed protecting. He began to have dark dreams. Hooded figures would appear in his dreams asking him to say, "Yes". Gavin would try to fight back but the figure would repeatedly sneer at him saying, "We are invited". Gavin was being pushed and rocked in his bed. There were banging and scratching noises around his home. There would be three knocks on the front door but, when Gavin answered the door, there would not be anyone there. These three knocks were a clear mocking of the blessed Trinity. This was also witnessed by case manager Jessie. Surviving on an average of two to three hours of sleep a night was taking its toll.

Gavin consulted with a fellow demonologist from America. Moe instantly advised Gavin to cleanse his home. Night after night Gavin performed deliverances with the help of Moe. Nothing appeared to be working. Moe suggested he should remove all haunted items from his home.

This had not occurred to Gavin as he was not even thinking straight at this time, as the infestation stage had now moved to oppression. Gavin felt he was having a mental breakdown.

These haunted objects included dolls, a rocking horse, mirrors, Ouija boards, voodoo kits and any amount of paranormal trigger objects. Gavin was advised to perform a ritual blessing on these objects and destroy them.

Meanwhile, Joseph's home was no better. The entity continued to keep Joseph awake at night by touching him. When Joseph would eventually sleep, the entity would travel into Helen's room. One night it began to growl like a dog at the end of her bed. This was terrifying for her. Joseph was still having dark dreams. He dreamt he was being pulled out of his bed, before waking up with a start. Helen was being scratched regularly. The entity extended its harassment to daylight hours. Joseph would feel it tapping on his shoulder aggressively. He could feel a hand grabbing him on his leg. If he sat down to relax, he could feel the back of the chair being thumped hard. This harassment and torment was endless.

It was now six months since their night of paranormal investigating, and four months since Gavin had first got involved in the case. At the end of April 2017, Gavin and

Jessie visited again. By this stage everyone was exhausted. The family were amazing. Every time Gavin and Jessie went to their home, Joseph and Helen would always be positive. Their resolve to end this nightmare was evident in how they were willing to try anything Gavin advised to get rid of this entity. Joseph had kept the journal as requested. Within this he described how the entity had become more aggressive. The taps to Joseph's body were getting harder and more defined. Sometimes Joseph could feel a finger being rubbed across his body. He could feel the weight of the entity on his bed. He could feel its heaviness. Exhaustion was what usually led him to drift off to sleep. On this occasion, the American demonologist Moe decided to speak to the family via Skype. As Gavin and the family spoke to Moe in the kitchen, Jessie sat alone in the sitting room. She had a headache and did not feel the best. As she sat there, she began to read through one of Gavin's books. She read some of the blessings used to rid demons to herself to pass the time. Gavin performed another clearing on the house and they both left.

On the way home Jessie complained of soreness on her shoulder and back but continued to drive. Once home, upon examination, there were seven large scratches running from her shoulder blade and down her back. They were so deep and red they looked like burn marks. At this stage, everyone was feeling the effects of this case; not just the family. Everyone was under attack.

The decision was made to remove and destroy the haunted objects and to contact an exorcist priest for help. Firstly the objects were removed and then ritually blessed and finally destroyed. These objects could never cause any other family harm.

Going through all of this has given Gavin a greater insight into what his clients go through. It has made him more determined to do whatever he can to help people who need him the most.

By May 2017, Jessie had got in contact with the

allocated exorcist priest. She explained to him everything that had been happening to Joseph and Helen and also what had been happening to Gavin. He agreed that this was now a case for him to deal with. By June word came that he was unwell but, as soon as he was better, he would do his best to help Joseph and Helen.

True to his word, he began the case. This exorcist priest was a lovely man who even met with Gavin and gave him a blessing. He advised Gavin to give up demonology as it is very dangerous.

Gavin has decided to continue to help people as much as he can for now, but is grateful for everything the priest did for him. We thought that was the end. We thought the priest would be able to free Helen and Joseph from this burden. In October 2017 the Church got back in contact with Jessie and informed Jessie that the exorcist priest was still involved with Joseph and his sister Helen.

Gavin and Jessie have visited Joseph and Helen in 2018. Since Gavin has left the case, the exorcist priest has visited the home on three occasions. He has said mass in the home and blessed both Helen and Joseph. Helen reports it appears to have backed away from her and she only gets the odd scratch now. It does, however, continue to torment Joseph. When he is in the bed, it hovers underneath and continues to touch him.

The exorcist priest believes he has done all he can at this stage, and another exorcist priest is being allocated to this case. They await his contact and the case remains open. Gavin and Jessie will continue to check in on Joseph and Helen and hope they can find some peace in their lives soon. They are a lovely family who do not deserve what is happening to them.

Once Pandora's Box is open, it is very hard to close. There has been a surge of people getting involved in paranormal investigations. They do it out of curiosity, desperate for proof that there is something out there. Or they do it for fun. It doesn't matter the reasons; it's the consequences that really matter. It is getting harder and harder to get rid of these entities which are just waiting for their opportunity to strike. Top exorcists in the Vatican in Rome will tell you it can take years of exorcism to free a person from these dark forces. So, the next time you think about giving up your free will and entering one of these locations you have got to ask yourself … are you prepared to face the possible consequences?

This is a story from someone I have been "friends" with on Facebook for a couple of years. He wishes to remain ANON, and that is good with me. This is a strange story and I wonder what you make of it? Again it is another one from Australia.

Australia's Melbourne Cup is a huge event, people coming from across the world to experience it. Back in 2003 a friend of mine, a jockey by the name of Kenny Dunlop, was working as a trainer. Known widely as the horse whisperer, he could work magic with the most difficult, seemingly hopeless cases.

He was a vibrant, outgoing, larger-than-life figure, who lit up a room the moment he entered it and was the life and soul of the party. A great friend, he was on your side 110% and would fight tooth and nail for you if he felt you'd been dealt a rough hand.

When he died, it was sudden, unexpected, and devastating. He was too young, too talented, too good a person to just give up on life. Yet it was not to be the last anyone heard from him.

His funeral was held in Melbourne, his memorial in South Australia. Obviously, his passion for working with horses was a focal point, and one particular horse was frequently mentioned, though the unusual name escaped most who attended the standing-room-only service; the only part people caught was 'Ma... Diva'. Everybody there wore something purple, Kenny's favourite colour – and it was a beautiful, sunny day.

At the end of the service, as everybody departed the chapel into the sunshine, rain suddenly crashed down on everybody, only ending when the last person was safe inside their car. More than one person said they heard Kenny laughing hysterically during the downpour.

What has this to do with the Melbourne Cup? Well, the weekend before the race, one of my sisters was looking through the paper, when it was swept off the table onto the floor and settled open to the page about the upcoming Cup and the excitement building around this one particular horse.

Makybe Diva.

Come race day, the entire family placed bets on 'Kenny's Horse' (as she has since and will forever be known), and cheered her on with as much gusto as we did when he raced Brutambo in the Easter Von Doussa Steeplechase years earlier. As the Diva crossed the line to screams of "You Beauty!" and "Come on, Kenny!" the jockey flung his arms into the air in celebration, and everyone stilled.

Kenny's face was the one caught in the camera lens; cheering the breathless win. A special piece on the news, 'The Tragedy Behind the Diva', told Kenny's story, and the owner of the training stables himself said that it was Kenny on the Diva's back as she crossed the finish line.

For three consecutive years, a history-making hat-trick, Makybe Diva won the coveted Cup, and each time Kenny's face flashed over that of the jockey's as horse and rider crossed the finish line.

The day before the race, I'd been uncertain whether I should place a bet, when Kenny's voice, clear as a bell as if he were sitting next to me in my lounge room, said, "She will make it a hat-trick sweetie, put money on her. You won't be sorry!"

He was right.

This is also from someone on Facebook called Herk Collins and he tells his story in a very matter of fact way. I don't think I would be so calm. He is part of the CSI Paranormal team from America.

I hardly know where to start. I have grown up with this all around me all the time. I've heard, seen, and felt so many things, from ice-cold hands on my shoulder to being punched in the stomach.

When I was about seven years old, I woke in the middle of the night and went down to the living room and took my bike out to ride just in front of my house. My mother came to the door telling me to get back in the house, but I really didn't want to; she then pointed behind me and told me louder to come in now. I turned to look and there was a smoky, black figure right behind me. I ran in the house and my mother stayed with me until I fell asleep. In my room, I never felt alone; I always had the sense that there were a lot of people, or whatever they were, in the room. I felt watched most of the time and always felt that someone or something would be there if I turned around.

Another time that I woke up in the middle of the night, I felt fearful and wanted my mom and dad; I couldn't see in their room as it was too dark. I went downstairs and, though it was dark, I called for my mom and dad and heard my dad say, "We're in here, son". I turned on the light and there was no one there at all. Now that the light was on, when I went back upstairs, I could see that my mom and dad were in bed asleep.

My family had a long history with the paranormal and we lived in a place that was once part of a cemetery. Some of the cemetery was still there and, depending on where you lived, you could see headstones when you look out your window. That was where my family lived when I was born and I grew up there, until my mom and dad passed. Many of the neighbours had activity in their homes as well.

I was in bed one night and heard what I thought was

my sister breathing loudly; she had asthma. I asked her the next day if she was the loud breathing I heard, she said she heard it too and thought it was me. A week or so later, I was alone and heard the heavy breathing again, and this time I could tell where it was coming from, it was the hall. I listened as the breathing got louder and closer, as though someone was coming toward me. It got louder and closer until whatever it was, was standing right in front of me breathing loud. I ran at the time, but these days things don't startle me like they used to.

I've seen things fly across the room, heard people talking in an empty room, and heard footsteps up and down the stairs and back and forth in the hall at night. Places I would go, strange things would happen, like things falling from the top shelf in a store as I walked down the aisle. I went into a convenience store to get a fountain soda, and as I got near it, the ice came pouring out as if someone put their cup to it to dispense the ice. As an investigator, I've been attacked by unseen hands after helping someone get rid of an evil spirit. This has happened twice.

My older brother was possessed when he was ten years old, he was never the same after his exorcism and when I was around thirteen he was once again becoming possessed. My sister saw it the first time, this time I saw it. He's no longer with us today; the demon ruined his life until he died.

I have been watching television and felt an ice-cold hand touch my shoulder, I've seen dead flowers floating toward me, and I've seen a full-bodied apparition several times in my life. When driving to my sister's house with a friend, I saw what I thought was a man standing in the middle of the road. I slammed on the brakes, thinking I was about to hit someone. When I stopped, it disappeared into the woods. It looked like a shadow but appeared as though it had a hat on; like a top hat and a long coat. I asked my friend if she saw it and she did, she then told me that she had been seeing shadows darting in and out of the woods for a short while, but didn't want to say anything, thinking it was just her.

When in my teens, my bedroom was across from the bathroom. I was lying in my bed taking a nap with my door open. My sister had gone into the bathroom and, when she came out, she said she saw a creature of some kind in my bed with long stringy hair, red eyes, and sharp-looking teeth. She got my mother and they woke me up and we all prayed because my mother was afraid that my brother's demon might be coming after me.

I was born into this life and I've been surrounded by the spirit world all my life. I began to study all I could about the paranormal when I was around fifteen and still do, as we never really learn all there is to learn; there is always so much more to discover. I've been in the field for thirty-three years and, though I'm now disabled, I still work with my team, but deal with the office end and helping people find closer teams in a hurry for what I feel are more serious situations. I'm the senior director for CSI Paranormal now and I think I will always be surrounded by the spirit world and, if that day comes, my kids may grow up the same way I did – for that reason, I'm glad I'm prepared and have much knowledge to give them.

Jon Kozuska is with the True North Paranormal team and has supplied this story for you. They are based in British Columbia, Canada and you can find out about them on Facebook.

The Vernon Towne Cinema

This was it, the first time Karina and I will be in front of a camera. I can tell you that we both were nervous and that is putting it mildly. This was a really 'I am Haunted' place, with lots of history and this was set to become a wild journey for us as True North Paranormal.

To put things in perspective, the Vernon Towne

Cinema's construction began in 1929 and she opened in 1930 and was a large part of the culture in Vernon, British Columbia, Canada. The venue saw generation after generation still contributing to be a go-to place to let loose and enjoy time with friends and family. In her beginning the building was a dance hall, housing many functions before continuing on her chain of evolution. The short version … this building has seen a lot!

Now, most buildings end up with stories of the paranormal; ghosts walking hallways, disembodied footsteps or voices and even a full apparition at times and the older they are the taller the tale becomes. However, every so often, as any paranormal investigator will tell you, the stories are true.

So we go back to where this story begins; the first filming of True North Paranormal. This building is misleadingly bigger than you would think, looking at it from the outside. Part of our process is a thorough walkthrough, looking for places to place the motion cameras which film in night vision; if there's evidence to catch, and the main cameras are not around, these little guys catch it. So, we naturally walk through, have the owner get their take on where the activity is so we can document and investigate, and this is where it all starts; a night we'd never forget.

We go to the upstairs of the theatre, a place that an apparition has been documented and seen by multiple people. One would assume there really isn't much to see, but I can assure you that these places have a lot going on behind the scenes. There's a narrow and steep staircase you take to go up onto the second floor and, once you reach the top, the atmosphere just changes.

While we listened to Hailee tell us the tale of the room we were standing in, you could just feel that we weren't alone. There's also a doorway that separates the projection room entrance from the large room we were standing in.

Hailee told us about all the strange happenings that

went on in the projection room, in addition to the office, where her father (and current owner) saw an apparition, and the electrical room. The fans in this room are loud – we had to speak in a raised voice just to hear each other – and, of course, the window; a small circular window that overlooks the theatre.

Our next stop was the theatre, the place where so many people have reported paranormal activity. Now the story went that the previous owner, Ellard, was a real mean guy. If you had your feet on the back of a seat and he caught you, you'd get slapped with a piece of rubber hose. The more we heard, the meaner he got, and that just adds to the already existing stories in place.

We made our way out of the theatre to a set of doors that led us down to the basement. Another set of eerie concrete stairs lead you down into the basement and it was here we got our first glimpse of what Ellard had in store for True North Paranormal throughout the evening. Hailee was telling us nothing ever happened in the basement – that it was always the main floor and second floor – and, as we were listening, we heard some heavy footsteps above us. These footsteps were heavy enough to make the boards above our heads creak with every step. They were loud enough I started looking around, but quickly turned my attention back to Hailee.

We left the basement and were at the double doors which were now closed; we most certainly didn't leave them that way. When we went to the basement we left them open; we didn't want to get locked in that stairwell … yet here they were, now closed. Hailee called her father, curious if he was in the building, but he was out and had been for some time. The front door was still locked. There was nobody but us in the building.

We and our producer, Dean Trumbley, and I, started placing the still cameras. I couldn't shake the footsteps, I had to know where they were, so, after we finished, I made my way back into the front entrance area – this was where the footsteps were – and I had to step hard to make them as loud as they were.

My wife, Karina, started filming her segment of our show with Dean Trumbley and Kent Mjtchie holding the cameras. Room by room, my wife went through the building speaking about what she felt in each of the rooms, the hallways and every nook and cranny. This gave me time to make sure the gear was ready to go. I made my way to nerve and got things ready and in place.

Karina returned and it was lights out time; my personal favourite part. The first room was the projection room. Karina and I began to ask questions, hoping for responses. Now this room – if we did get a response, well, we wouldn't know, it was so loud in there! Looking at footage later, almost every time Hailee walked past the motion camera, there was one single orb that would follow. We all felt that we were going to get something, just where and when?

We went to the theatre next; with all the reports I was beyond excited to get into this one. Karina made her way to the front of the theatre with the FLIR thermal camera in tow. She was filming her segment up front, while I was in the back of the theatre working on a spot that Karina had singled out. When she does this, she's pretty bang on and typically we don't second guess. A minute or so into her filming, the tablet that started out at 100 per cent charge when she turned it on goes dead; the power drained completely out of it – and, as we all know, this is a sign of things to come. I was doing my best to draw out Ellard and get him to show himself; somehow tell us he was there. I was getting some readings on the MEL meter, but that was the extent of it.

We packed up: Dean first, then Karina; followed by me, leaving Kent Mjtchie and camera two behind. We were talking, going over the FLIR situation, when we heard a bang. Kent made his way out of the theatre and was white; he told us he just watched a seat slam itself down right in front of him. We were intrigued so we were naturally going back again; the building was coming alive and we were in the middle of it.

We made our way up the stairs, unloaded some SD cards at nerve, and back out we went. It was time to go to the room behind the projection room, the one up the narrow and steep staircase which also had a death related to it. We set up some ghost boxes along the rail; Karina had the FLIR in tow again with a fresh charge and I had the spirit box, a tool I love because I always seem to get a response with it. Dean gave us a signal and the camera was rolling, time to go to work.

We made our way to the middle of the room asking generalized questions. Karina is locked on the stairs, not taking her eyes from them, swearing she saw a head pop up and back down. She raises the FLIR and a strange and unexplained light anomaly was present. I turned my attention that way, asking yet more questions, "Can you turn those lights on?", and did we get a response! The lights slowly started getting bright, a sign of a response to say the least.

I asked if the entity could make them brighter, saying, "Do you know how?" And a very snarky response came through: "Can you?" Not only were we dealing with an intelligent haunting, but we were also dealing with an attitude, it would seem! The light on the FLIR vanished without a trace and there were no more responses that followed; almost like the entity had moved to a different area.

I need to add here: there is a back room with a door at the end of this room. It was in this room, with my hand-held camera on me, we saw orbs. Clear as day, no nucleus, it was an orb and the pattern they moved in was so fast. Thank goodness for night vision. It was one of those rare moments which makes doing what we do that much more rewarding.

We decided, since the building was so alive, it was time

to revisit the theatre; provoke Ellard into giving us a reaction – and we got one. We made our way back in, set up, had ghost boxes on some of the chairs. I went to the front this time, Karina was at the back. Kent and I began filming me while Dean and Karina worked the back; it just felt like something was going to happen – you just get that vibe. A little bit through my segment, Karina and Dean called me; one of the ghost boxes were lighting up. I made my way up there with the MEL meter in my hand, looking for changes in the environment. The place really was alive now, I made my way to the front to finish my filming with Kent and was really provoking, doing my best to get that crucial response we all want, almost as if to give validation. Karina and Dean start making their way to the front of the theatre, and it was dark I may add. The only light you can see is the light that comes from the view screen on the camera, barely enough to illuminate. Karina sits in some chairs so as not to get in my camera's view and Dean is walking down a row when again, SLAM another chair slams down right behind Dean. It made us all jump, what a display! Dean managed to get from the centre of a row of seats to the aisle in about seven steps; now I work close with Dean during investigations and I have to tell you that he rarely jumps, let alone moves that fast. Ellard was very much with us and making it so we knew it. All the events that led up to this point, the slow building into this huge loud aggressive slamming of a seat (which I did everything in my power to debunk and discredit, I may add, with no successful explanation whatsoever) gave us concrete proof that this building WAS haunted.

We packed up, buzzing from what we experienced; what a great night full of activity. Amongst the laughing and the joking, and the overall thrill we had all experienced, we really could not have asked for a better first time in front of the camera. We thanked Hailee for her time and the access to the building, packed up the cars and went for breakfast before heading home. I'll tell you this much, for all of us the conversation centred around the evidence we collected, almost without effort.

This theatre is genuinely haunted and, if you're ever in Vernon, B.C., Canada, take the time to catch a movie here. You will be in a historical building that's seen so much and be in the middle of a ghost story – there really is no place like the Vernon Towne Cinema.

Until next time … keep it creepy!

This is a story from Keeley Thornton and another story sourced from social media pages. She is from the UK and this is one of the strangest I have ever heard!

OK, well when I was about five years old in the early 1980s, we lived in a Victorian house in a place called Copperas House, Todmorden. I don't remember when it began, I just remember the girl being there. The house was on the side of the canal; the front of the house was on the main road and the back of the house was on the canal bank. The way the house was set up was: you walked in the front door and ahead of you there was a long corridor, at the end was the kitchen; just before that on the right were the stairs and, next to the stairs, also on the right, was the front room. So, to go between the kitchen and the front room you passed the stairs.

I would, as a small child, frequently sit on the bottom step "talking" to someone who I called "Fluey". I could see her; she was a small child like me, may be about five or six, she had blond hair, a pinafore dress and she was coloured pale blue. She had Cupid bow lips and looked pretty. I don't remember how I knew, but I knew she died from influenza. My mum would be in the kitchen and she would hear me talking to her, hearing just my side of the conversation. She would come past and quite crossly say, "Stop it! Just stop it! There's no one there!" I remember not understanding why she couldn't see her.

Anyway, my biggest memory of Fluey was being upstairs and she asked if I wanted to fly? Being a small child this seemed like a very exciting thing to do. She said, "Take my hand and we will fly downstairs!" So I did. I remember lifting off my feet, and floating through the air, seeing the base step to the attic stairs as we floated gently down past it. As we neared the bottom steps, my mum came out of the kitchen to go into the front room. Fluey at that moment let go and disappeared. I consequently dropped the last two steps, landing in a heap at the bottom, laughing hysterically at the fun I had just had, but my mum, with absolute horror, thought I'd just fallen down the whole flight! But also couldn't understand why I was laughing and hadn't a mark on me. I don't remember much more of when I was that age, but it would be a few years before anything else paranormal happened.

Krisanne Pozo is a friend of Brian Holloway who also lived in Gibraltar and advised me to get in touch with her as she had some interesting stories to tell. Here is one of them. If any of you want an interesting place to visit, Gibraltar (also called The Rock), certainly fulfils that criteria; it has amazing history that goes back a very long way.

My husband and I organize Ghost Hunts and paranormal events in Gibraltar. Those that do not know Gibraltar will not understand the history within Gibraltar: our Rock consists of lots of tunnels which were dug out by the military during the war; here men used to live inside these tunnels and spent years working within them. There were hospitals and operating theatres too.

One night we had a group of people visiting the World War Two tunnels up the Rock. We divided the group in two, the first group stayed with the medium in a room called the generator room, and the second group came with me to the hospital and operating rooms.

We formed a circle; I stood in the middle and started calling out. We soon all felt the temperature drop. As I called out, "Is there anybody here with us? Please make a noise so we all know," the temperature in the room became very cold and we heard a stomping sound. I called again, "If this was you, please stomp again but twice." Again my question was answered with two stomping sounds. I started asking more questions, "Please show us more, throw a stone," again a stone was thrown in the corner of the room. The atmosphere changed again; we could see how cold it was as, when I spoke, you could see the condensation appearing. Everyone felt uneasy and quite scared.

Our medium sensed that something was going on as he entered the room moments later; he came up to me, saw what was happening and then stood at the corner of the room where all the noises were coming from. He was quiet for a while and then started moaning. I realised he was either possessed or in trance, as all he kept saying was, "Help me, help me." I asked who he was, and he said, "I'm a soldier reporting for duty!" He then started shuffling his feet and walking towards me looking very angry. I knew I could not panic as I had a group of twenty people around me, trusting that I would keep them safe. So, I shouted, "Stop, soldier!" A few paces away from me, the medium just dropped to the floor, and we all saw this shadow running towards the tunnels and we even heard the footsteps running! Just when he got out of sight, a member of the first group, which was nowhere near us and completely unaware of what was happening, shouted that he had seen a soldier running past them and most people also heard his footsteps!

This is a bit of a coup on my part I think. As I said in the introduction, I gathered all these great stories from social media. I was lucky to have connected with one of the most famous ghost hunters of them all. I asked for stories from him, as I had with all of the others, never thinking in a million years he would have time. But here are two stories that he gave for you to enjoy, all in his own words.

There is almost nothing else that divides believers, sceptics, paranormal investigators, non-investigators, everyone, right down the middle. Now what I am talking about is Ouija boards.

By the way, my name is Robb Demarest and I have been officially investigating the paranormal for almost thirty years. When we say paranormal, of course we are talking about all sorts of things from ESP, telekinesis to the Loch Ness Monster, Big Foot, ghosts, demons; all those things that don't fit into any other category.

In this story I would like to talk about one of those categories, and the one thing that divides everyone, and that is the Ouija board. Is it a toy? Is it a gimmick? We know that it has something to do with our subconscious moving the planchette – i.e. the small marker that you place on top of the board with all the letters of the alphabet – but some people will say "no, no, it is much more. It is a dark doorway to demons and darkness that you can never come back from. It is dangerous and should be avoided at all costs". And yet, there it is for sale at my local pharmacy! Nowadays, they make you show ID to buy pills to make you go to sleep. But, any twelve-year-old kid can go in and buy this portal to hell!

Well, I've never told these stories before and I've got two. There is more, but this time I want to tell two short stories about my experiences with the Ouija board.

Now, as someone who never put much stock in it, I went with the theory that your brain unknowingly sends a signal to your hands; that you are moving the board even though you would pass a polygraph swearing you are not, because you don't think you are.

OK, well, I was about twelve – maybe thirteen – years old, I was with my two cousins in their house, which was empty at the time, and they said, "Hey wait a second; we saw Mum and Dad the other night by candlelight and they were using a Ouija board".

I knew what a Ouija board was, but I had never used one. They said they were asking for Lottery numbers – found out later that is supposedly something you should never do, but so be it. So, I said, "Do you think we should try it?" Well, come on, you've got a twelve-year-old, a thirteen-year-old and a fourteen-year-old, damned right we're going to try it! So, we made sure their mum and dad were nowhere to be seen and we snuck up and we took their old, dusty 1960s Ouija board down.

We put our hands on it and said, "Are we supposed to light candles?" It seemed kinda odd as it was about 2 pm, so we said, "Nah! We'll skip the candle part." I can't speak for them, but I will say that my heart was going a little faster – you know, the expectation was there – but as the seconds ticked by … nothing happened! It didn't move an inch. We looked at each other and said, "Are we supposed to say something? Are we supposed to say some sort of incantation, some sort of spell? How in hell are you supposed to kick-start this thing?" There is no GO button; it's just a piece of plastic, a board with letters on it … and then it moved. So, of course as with every Ouija board session done in existence, we all looked around and said to each other, "You did it", "No, you did it!", "No I didn't do it, I know you did though!" The recriminations flew back and forth and back and forth. Then it moved again. This time we were all kinda quiet because we were in the midst of arguing and not even paying attention, so the plastic indicator was sliding on its own! Granted, our fingers were on it, but only lightly. So we started arguing and once again, it moved, but only slightly.

Now, I'd seen it on TV and they had seen their parents use it. This thing moves around the board, moving to numbers and spelling out names and telling stories, but for us it moved maybe a quarter of an inch three times. I said,

"Ah! I think it is all bunk!" and at that exact moment when I said it, there was a piercing scream from a woman within that house, which we knew was empty! That house had never shown any signs of being haunted, no one had seen anything, heard anything, but we all heard that scream! Then there was that moment, we immediately took our hands off that friggin' piece of plastic, and that lasted for about 0.3 seconds, followed by shoving the damned table out of the way and running for the door like the devil himself was chasing us!

Now of course, the postscript is that you have to go home again, and we did a few minutes later but thinking, you know, what if by some possibility there was someone in danger somewhere around the house? Bearing in mind we lived on one hundred acres, so we thought it unlikely that there would be someone there, but we went room by room, inch by inch throughout the house. We didn't find anything to have made that scream.

So – on to story number two.

I attended boarding school, not many people know that, it was in a small town in Connecticut. One of the other dormitories had a Ouija board. I said, "I don't mess with that stuff, I know where that goes!" And they were using it to predict the outcomes of lacrosse games, and it was surprisingly accurate. So, my room-mate came back from vacation, he lived down here in Florida, and he said, "Hey, I've got a Ouija board, we can try it out." So, I said, "Sure, the first time was a fluke." So, down our fingers went again.

Once again the seconds ticked by, this time the minutes ticked by, to the point we said, "This is stupid! We've got to get up early for breakfast tomorrow." So, we put the board back in its box and we put the planchette on top of it, and we put it in the closet.

Well, in the middle of the night something hits me in the back. I said, "What the Hell?" I reached behind me and

I could feel the outline; it was the damned Ouija board! So, I take the Ouija board and throw it back in the closet and I called my room-mate several names that we won't repeat here. He wakes up and swears that I had been sleeping and also that I was an idiot and other words we shall not repeat. So, I said, "OK, I'm going to prove it." I jumped out of the bed, I was actually in the top bunk; he was at the bottom. I jumped out and went over and throw the light on. First thing I do, I look in the closet … and there is a problem.

The Ouija board is back in the box perfectly, with the planchette on top of it. I know I threw the board into the closet. But, there is my room-mate saying, "I told you, idiot." So, as I turned to go back to bed, I looked and said, "Then what the fuck is this?" I showed him my back, where there was a deep red line running across my back.

Paul Jackson is another Canadian who was good enough to send these stories for us, he is from Ontario and his details can also be found on Facebook.

It was early in the 1980s I would have been fifteen – sixteen years old at the time. The town was called Queensville in the township of East Gwillimbury; the town most famous for the abduction of young school girl Christine Jessop.

I lived in a century home on the main street of the town; we had a small barn in the back yard that my friends and I claimed as our spot, more or less. We would have snowmobiles and dirt bikes in the barn all year round. We began noticing that tools and small things would go missing, but we never thought too much about it. One evening my parents had gone out and left myself at home with a couple friends, we decided to go out to the barn and move a bunch of cardboard boxes upstairs and staple them over the cracks in the boards, to cut down on the wind coming through and make it a little warmer for us to hang out.

I picked up a tall lamp (no shade) and put it through the one foot square hole we had in the middle of the floor. The whole barn was approximately 25'x35' in size. As I placed the light through the hole in the floor to light up the upper level, I looked at my buddies and told them to pass me the folded boxes and I'd go up the stairs and throw them up. I made my way to the stairs and started walking up them. The very second my head was level with the floor above there were very LOUD footsteps; seemed to be stomping across the floor towards me. Dirt was falling between the cracks in the floor and I jumped off the stairs and the three of us panicked and rushed out the doors.

We ran to the front of the house out by the roadway. Both the barn doors were wide open on the front of the barn; the four-pane window above the door was illuminated still by the light I had put up through the floor. I suggested that we walk quietly around the rear of the barn and on the second floor there is a large window that we should be able to see inside, and see who is there.

We make our way around and, looking up at the window, there was a green turtle pool (kid's pool) leaning against the window, blocking our line of sight. However, with the light behind we could make the outline of what appeared to be shape and size of a large person. We ran back around the front of the barn to the road again, trying to figure out what to do next. There was a stray cat that lived in the barn and we could never get it to leave, when suddenly this cat came flying out of the barn as if it was on fire, running onto the roadway past us and being hit by a car right in front of us.

Now I was mad! I cursed "F… this" I said, and started back to the barn. I walked in, picking up the pitchfork and walking towards the stairs; as I got about 10' from the stairs, again BOOM, BOOM, BOOM! Heavy footsteps! I ran back out and I turned and pushed the doors shut and locked them with the hook.

Now nobody could get out of the barn unless they were to break a board, the doors or the window. We regrouped at the front of the house and, looking up at the window in the barn, we see a black head and shoulders lean and look through the bottom windowpane, seemingly looking out at us.

Now the three of us, obviously shaken and seeing what we have seen, were deciding who was going to call the cops and report this. The reason we wanted to involve the police is because, just a short time before this, a young schoolgirl by the name of Christine Jessop was abducted and killed just down the road and we were concerned because nobody had been caught for the murder and everyone in town was on edge, not knowing who or where this person might be, so we thought maybe this is that person!

As we stood there trying to decide who was going to go call, I said I would stay and keep an eye on the barn to make sure nobody comes out. We looked back up at the window and this time the head and shoulders appeared on the other side, looking out at us again. As we all saw it I pointed and said, "Look"! That instant, the light went out. Even though the light was about 15' from the window … to see the figure and the light to go out instantly, there is no way it could have reached over and turned it off.

My buddies went and made the call about what was going on. The police arrived, they listened to what we told them then they told us to stay at the front of the house. The two officers approached the barn quietly; guns drawn they made their way in and through the barn with their flashlights on. We could see the lights through the boards, and they came back out a few minutes later saying there was NOBODY in the barn and no broken windows or boards. With that, the one officer asked if the well pipe was always upstairs coiled on the floor? We said yes it was and he said that nobody could "run" across the floor without tripping. We know what we saw in the barn that night and we experienced many other paranormal things in the barn and the house after this for several years. Had the two barn doors fly open and hit me in the face in the dead of winter around 12am with temps around about minus twenty, no wind at all, after making fun of "it" on our way to the barn. Have had several things happen in the house as well if you would like any of that.

I contacted a lady on Twitter called Sammy Rawlinson from the UK, who was eager to let you all read her story. She is a psychic medium and, although I am quite sceptical regarding those in this field, I must say that after speaking to her about myself (she does not know me at all) I was quite impressed with what she had to tell me. So, whatever your views about this subject, please enjoy this one.

After asking Sammy how old she was when she first realized she had this gift, this is what she said.

"I was only about five; it was very early in my life. I didn't see spirits until a lot later on. It was just thoughts and dreams at first. I would dream about things and in the future they really happened. I didn't know straight away that was what it was.

As I got older I didn't get any help in developing what I can do as my mum, her mum and even mum were all psychic mediums, so they all knew what I was experiencing, and it was just a normal thing to them. My dad was a hardened sceptic, so I had the two forces in the same place.

I have now got to the point where this is something I can turn off, although when I was young, it was a constant thing that was always there. I can now open my mind to give someone a Tarot reading and then turn it off at the end. It takes a long time to be able to do that, it is a very hard thing to get the hang of doing."

I asked Sammy what people think or say when they find out that she has this ability.

"I think they think that I'm insane! They think I'm a lunatic, but then I try and prove it to them and let the work do all the talking! I look on this as both a curse and a blessing, as everything in life is neither black nor white; there are a lot of grey areas too. I think it is the intention behind the user which makes it good or bad. That's what I think. I don't ever think I could use a Ouija board; they are too risky in my view, you could open a portal and not know how to close it again. There is no way I would use one."

"I have actually seen a demon. One night, I was about eighteen at the time, my friends and I went to a party at someone's house. I got really ill after that night and that was the night I managed to get a photo of the twelve-foot-tall demon. It is on Facebook if you want to have a look at it. It is a shadow that just doesn't belong there. I don't look on them as necessarily evil; I just look on them as a ghost or a spirit."

"The first time I ever saw a ghost, I was at my friend's house and we were drinking, and she was going to be eighteen at midnight (which I now know is the time spirits visit us on birthdays and anniversaries). I didn't know this at the time as I was only eighteen too."

"Sadly, her dad had committed suicide a few years earlier, although we were not talking or thinking about anything like that at the time. We were just enjoying the evening and having fun. Before she went to bed she made me a bed in the living room and we sat there talking for a while then and I began to see a silvery cloud-like thing starting to appear in the room. It seemed to glisten, and I thought, "What the hell is that?" Even though I saw things in the future, I had never seen an actual ghost! It started to form in the shape of a face, my friend was still talking, and I was just thinking, "What is it I am seeing there?" It started to form quicker into a man's face and it came right up to my face and I was trying to push it back. It came even closer and I couldn't push back any further and I was really scared now. My friend was still just sat there talking! My stomach was turning over, he looked like he was wearing a type of cowboy hat and smoking a cigar. Then he just appeared to evaporate. I shot out of the bed and I was trying to get out of the house. My friend said, "Sammy, what's the matter?" I said "I just want to go home. Get your mum to take me home, I want to go home now!" Her mum had had a drink too so she couldn't drive. I was in such a state, and it took quite a while for me to calm down enough to tell her what had happened. She asked me what it had looked like and I described to her what I had seen and what had happened. When I told them about the cowboy hat and cigar, her mum said, "Oh my God! It sounds just like her dad used to look!" She went and got some photos out and, in the photograph, well, I couldn't believe what I was seeing. He had a hat similar to a cowboy hat on and a cigar! I remember it so well and so vividly, as that was my first proper experience of seeing a ghost."

"I was really confused after seeing this and I told my mum and all she said was, "Oh yes, that is how it happens." She was so matter-of-fact about it, like it was all normal to her. I don't think I have ever seen another as clearly, as it was so physically in the room, and I will always remember that it was precisely on the stroke of twelve. I will never forget as it was so scary!"

"I also get premonitions and one of the ones I most remember was that I was dreaming I was on a pushbike and I remember dreaming that I fell off it and I had cut my arms and legs and I was really bleeding and I was crying. Then I realized I was dreaming and I woke up and didn't think any more of it. A short while later my friend came round and she had a moped. It sounds stupid now, we were about seventeen. I shouldn't have got on, she didn't have a licence, she'd been drinking and we were silly kids.

Anyway, the inevitable happened and she crashed it; we both came off it and thankfully although we did get hurt, it wasn't seriously. I remember looking down at myself at my arms and legs and I was bleeding! I remembered the dream, although in the dream it was a pushbike."

"I now know that it is always very muddled with premonitions. Like for instance you could have a fight with someone in a dream and then it happens in real life but the person changes, but this one is one that always sticks out to me. We always call them warnings from the other side. Like you could hear a song in a dream and when you put the radio on it is playing, things like that happen often to me. I have always been bigger on premonitions than psychic."

"One of them I had when I was just a child. I was out on a school trip to Northern Village in Stockton where I live. I remember looking at the sky and it was bright and sunny, but I saw a thunder bolt and rain, and I said to the teacher, "At least when it starts thundering we can stand under that tree." She looked at me as if I was a bit odd. I think it was about five minutes later the heavens opened and there was a big storm, and we all ran for cover of the tree. The teacher started at me with a very peculiar look and must have been thinking that that was a bit weird!"

"There was another amazing one I thought I might tell you about. I see stuff every day, but the biggest one for me was when I was learning to become a medium, which was later on in my life. I was told I had to have a spirit guide, and I thought, "I can't have a spirit guide, I've never seen one!" Mum said, "You don't see them until you learn." I really wanted to see my spirit guide, I had seen her in my mind's eye, and now know she's called Helen, and she has red hair. I was meditating and was deep in the trance and I was begging, "Please, please let me see you. I really want to see you!" She was showing herself in my mind, but I was needing so badly to "see" her for real. I must have been begging for about twenty minutes! You know, you are so excited to get to see her."

"This for me is one of the most real paranormal experiences I have ever had. I was sitting on my bed and I was blindfolded, so I didn't have any visual distractions and I suddenly had a funny, fuzzy kind of feeling coming over me. I thought, "Something is happening." Suddenly, even though I was blindfolded, I could clearly see the room. I saw my bedroom door open and it looked like a gold ball of light entered the room, but it was about half the size of a person! I thought, "WOW!" then the door shut again, and everything went black. I was very scared, and I could feel there was something in the room with me. I thought, "Take the blindfold off" but I had just been begging my guide to show herself to me and she had. I was so scared to take the blindfold off, and I could feel the presence getting heavier and heavier and then I started to shake. I know now that is the "calling card" that my guide is working with me or at least near me. I took the blindfold off and it was amazing! I will never forget it, as I physically saw this golden ball of light!"

This is a story from a very nice lady called Tracy Cooper-Stevens. I met her through Facebook and she had a few great things to share; the first being that she is a direct descendent of one of the Pendle Witches, one who was an aunt many generations ago. Apart from that she owns the Lancashire Paranormal Investigations team, in the UK.

My first experience of the paranormal came when I was about six years old. My parents had taken me to visit some relatives who had the family farm on Pendle Hill (where my aunt and the others accused of witchcraft lived in the 1600s).

The farm had lots of out-buildings and in one of the small barns I kept a collection of Barbie dolls on a shelf. They were always there so I could play with them whenever I visited. So I was playing and then I got called in for dinner. I left the dolls all sitting very nicely around the small tea set that was there too. After we had eaten, I went back to the barn and got very upset as all the dolls, who had been sitting up enjoying their tea party, were now laying all face down and two had even had their heads pulled off! There was no one about except me and I know I didn't do it. Suddenly, right next to my ear, I heard a voice distinctly say, "It's all right!" I spun round and there was no one there. With that I ran back to the house to tell them what I saw and what I'd heard and my grandmother said, "Don't worry, it was only your aunt and she won't hurt you!" That I will always remember, and I suppose was my start on this path.

My team and I heard about a street in Accrington which seems to have an enormous amount of paranormal activity; there have been many deaths in the street and it works out to be about ten a year. There are shops lining the street and we went to one, being an antique shop. The owner had contacted us to say she was having problems with things moving on their own and footsteps were heard when there was only herself in the shop.

I went there on my own the first time, just to meet with the owner and speak to her to find out more, and see for myself what I would be getting the team involved with. As I went in, I was surrounded by items that must have spanned at least two hundred years. Being a paranormal investigator, my first thought was that some of these objects could have something attached to them, as there are many items on record that have this problem. I did feel an atmosphere that was totally different to that outside, it was almost heavy.

The owner came and met me and we got to talking about the things she had been experiencing. She did say that she had been "talking" to whatever it was there by using a Ouija board. I told her she must stop using that immediately, as I believe that when you use one of them, you do open a doorway to the other side and if it is not closed properly, who knows what you might let come through it? We talked a little longer, and the feeling I got from the premises made me certain that it was worth my team coming to do an investigation, and to see what we could find out for her. It turned out that it wasn't just her shop, but there were about fifteen others in the street that had, or were having, paranormal problems too.

My team and I arrived and started to set up cameras, and we are a team that make use of as much tech as we can, so recorders for EVP's, thermal cameras and much more. We started by doing a sweep to find out if there were any abnormal electrical readings and, if there were, find the cause. Everything was fine. As the night wore on, we did get a few EVP's that were quite distinct, one saying, "Get out!"

My partner Mike is the tech guy, and he went upstairs to take down the CCTV camera he had placed at the top of the stairs. Just as his head reached over the top stair, he saw a pair of old black boots and the person was wearing what looked like an old duffle coat, although he could only see the boots and to the hem of the coat. He rushed back down and came in to tell us what he had seen. We all went straight back with him and as we got to the landing, of course, there was nothing to see. We stood there while he was taking the camera down, looking for anything out of the ordinary. Suddenly he said "I don't feel very good." And with that, he went as white as a sheet and slipped sideways. If there hadn't been another male member of the team there at the time, he would have fallen straight down the stairs. As it was, he managed to catch him before he fell and laid him out on the floor. His eyes were open and he was breathing all right, but apart from that he was totally unresponsive. He was that way for at least ten minutes and then he began to come back to his senses. All he remembered was not feeling great, and nothing else. Of course, we left as soon as we could after that.

We went there about four or five times in total, every time we got EVPs and, one night, we were sitting and I looked at one of the meters I had put on the table and the thing was moving, all on its own. There was no one touching the table and this thing was moving; everyone was stunned. We had seen other things move out of the corner of our eyes, but this was definite movement right in front of us.

Sadly, not long after this, the owner of the shop died. There was a post mortem conducted and the cause of death was listed as "unknown".

On checking out the history of the area, as we always do with any location we visit, we found that at the beginning of the last century there had been a very old graveyard at the end of the road, which dated back to five or maybe six hundred years ago. This had been built over as the town got busier and there is also a river which runs to the side of the street, which now heads towards a car park. In my experience, it seems that whenever there is water near, the possibility of paranormal activity increases.

As I said before, there are maybe fifteen shops or other premises which have paranormal activity in the same street, not all seem to be harmless. There is a man seen walking up the road, dressed like the man my partner saw; many people have seen him and he gives off a very evil feeling when seen. It seems to be the general consensus of opinion locally that he was what we would call, in these days, a pimp. He would go to the local pubs and rooms and get his cut of the prostitute's earnings and, if they didn't pay up, they would get severe beatings. There is also a pub at the end of the road where it is rumoured that a young woman hung herself, it is said that she was having an affair with a local monk many years ago and the affair was discovered.

Personally, I feel that the whole of the street is being visited by something more than just the man. I don't know how best to describe it except to say that I don't think it is a human spirit or spirits that are causing so many unexplained deaths in the buildings on this street. It is something far more than that. I feel the whole street needs a clearing or exorcism of some sort; this may be the only way to put an end to the tragedies they are experiencing.

These next offerings are from Simon Smith and again, as all the others in this book, I met him through social media sites. He is part of Sussex Paranormal; he has worked with some very well-known people in the paranormal world in the past, although I shall not mention them here. His team also do many fund-raising events. I hope you enjoy his stories.

A friend called Dave Warner and I went to investigate at Michelham Priory in Sussex, a very large old manor house which at one point was given to Anne of Cleves by Henry VIII. Many of you may have seen it on *Most Haunted* as they did a show there. This time we had BBC Southern Counties at the Priory, who were recording it with us. It had been organized by a medium friend of mine called Karen; it was a public event, and anyone interested in the paranormal could purchase a ticket for the event. However, she had some places left and this is why I had been asked if I would like to go. We were separate from the public group and we went and did our own small investigation.

It was the second time I had been there and, on the way up the staircase, there is a priest hole where the Roman Catholic priests used to hide away from those who came looking for them during the Dissolution. Many of the clergy had to stay in those tiny, cramped spaces for hours, or maybe even days, on end. Dave went down into the small space and took with him the camera man, and quite clearly the camera's microphone picked up the sounds of a baby crying.

At these types of investigations, we always try to keep each group on the same level, so if we hear a noise upstairs or in another part we are not in, we know that it is none of us who have made the sound. On this occasion, all the teams were upstairs. There is a long flight of stairs with a large landing at the top with rooms off it, then just a few steps up to a long hallway, with two rooms off to the left and the same to the right. In front is what is known as the family room. It had been turned into a nursery room, although I don't think it was originally used for the purpose, it had just been set up that way in more modern times, with a baby's cradle and a few other things a baby would have used in those days.

A friend called Troy and I decided we wanted to do some filming in there. There were also a couple more people in there with us, a friend called Mike and his wife who were filming what we were doing. Mike, I should say, is an open-minded sceptic. There were also two mediums with us that night although they were not with us in the room, but at the other end of the priory; they were called Karen and Ann, and they were with the public team. They were also on the same level as us, but they were a good way away from us, as we and they were doing our own investigations.

Troy and I were filming in the nursery; we had the door shut at the time. About ten minutes into what we were doing we heard a commotion from outside the room, so we opened the door to find out what was going on. What had happened was one of members from the public group had been shining a torch along the hallway, although he didn't see anything; there were two women with him who were looking around and down at the stairs. They were the ones who saw a translucent woman hitch up her long skirt and walk up the stairs, along the hallway and up the small flight of stairs into the room that Troy and I had been filming in! We had seen nothing; no one had come into the room while we were there. Mark (the sceptic) did say after, that if you had waved a hand in front of her face when they saw her that she would have ignored them; they got the impression that she was totally unaware of the investigators who were in the house at the time. The mediums that were with their group saw nothing either, in fact they were a bit gob-smacked. I remain a bit sceptical of mediums and their abilities anyway, but who am I to judge?

I have been to the priory many times since and every time you go, the feeling is different. If I remember rightly, the year this happened was 2006, although I can't be sure. In the end we went ten or twelve times during that year, although it may have only been two or three times we actually had anything of any significance happen to us.

One other thing that happened there was when I was alone, although there were other members of the team in different parts of the building. I was hosting a charity event there, as my team often do, although not always at the same place. I remember I wasn't feeling too well at the time and I said to the team that I wasn't feeling too great and would they mind doing what was needed while I went and got some fresh air, which I did. This was probably about half past three/four in the morning. I went out the front door into the grounds, I had shut the front door as the other guys were doing their vigils and I didn't want to interrupt them. There was a space where we all parked our cars and behind them was a small field with old barns in. It was here I thought I saw a flash of blue light out of the corner of my eye. I looked over and saw nothing to have caused it. As I looked away, I thought I saw another flare of blue light and I heard someone shouting really loud, although I couldn't make out what it was they were saying but it was coming closer and closer. Then it stopped and I couldn't hear anything else and saw no more lights.

In the morning when it got light, I looked out and saw that it was all just farm land; there was no reason for me to have seen what I did. There were houses a way off, but they were in the opposite direction. I know I wasn't feeling too good at the time, but I know it wasn't me hallucinating!

Another story I have for you happened when a friend of mine, Simon Coleman, who is a roof tiler, got a contract to mend the roof of a very old listed building in Guildford in Surrey which was owned by the local council. The property had been lived in and over the years had been modernised in a fashion, but the council wanted to have it put back into its more original state. There had been various workmen there and there was scaffolding around it while the works to restore it were being carried out.

We had got permission to investigate there and we only ever went in small groups, maybe five or six of us at a time. It had been occupied by an elderly couple and the man had died and his wife had gone into a home. Simon had picked up the contract to re-roof the property; it was built in the fifteenth/sixteenth century, and he is a specialist when it comes to property of that age. He obviously got talking to other tradesmen who were working there, and they all told him that there was a strange feeling in the house, so much so that one guy said he wouldn't work there anymore if he had to be alone there. It had a strange layout too, but one thing which sticks out to me was the fact that up the top of the stairs, rather than put wallpaper up, they had cut random pictures out of magazines and glued them onto the wall.

Either the first or second time we went there, there were only four of us: Simon and his wife; and myself and my wife (now ex!). The three of them went out of the house for a smoke break and left me inside where I was setting up the video camera. All of a sudden, right in my ear, I heard a very wheezy breath! I knew I wasn't imagining it as when we played the camera back, you could hear it on there too, very distinctly. I looked around as soon as I heard it and there was nothing there that I could see. I thought, "Well! That was strange!" Or words to that effect, if you know what I mean. That was quite an unnerving thing to have happen, when you're all alone in the house. It did get the adrenalin pumping a bit! It was at that investigation we captured pictures of a few distinct orbs too.

My wife at the time and I went back one day with a very well-known psychic medium, who has been on TV many times, although I won't mention his name, and he went around the house. At the end of his tour around, he told me that he never wanted to set foot in the building again! I believe in spirits, but not really mediums, it just doesn't seem real to me what they do. But, that is just my opinion.

About six of us went there again one evening; there was still work going on and scaffolding around the building, but the house was secure and always shut up at the end of the work day. Simon had the key and we went in, did our filming and whatever we had to do; we left everything alone and didn't cause any damage, we left everything as we had found it. On this evening we had been there for about four hours. My friend Mark was there with me, he was also the one who had seen the ghost at Michelham Priory; we were all of us in the front room and taking down the equipment to pack away, when we heard from upstairs an almighty BANG! There were very loud stomping footsteps and somebody shouting, although it was impossible to make out what they were saying, but they were sounding very angry. I got an awful feeling at that time; I can't explain it except that it felt like dread. It takes quite a lot to worry me, or scare me, but that made me feel very uncomfortable. I admit it – I was scared.

We all went upstairs as we thought it might be someone who had maybe broken in and perhaps were a bit deranged, as the only way in up there was up the scaffolding. Everything was shut up and safe and secure as it should be. I just didn't want to stay there any longer. I was still feeling very uneasy in the house. I got the feeling it didn't want me there, so I thought, "I'm not taking a chance, I'm going home early!" So I did. As it often happens, we were putting all the gear away at the time, so nothing was caught on camera or recorded. I went back once more after that night, but nothing happened that time.

Another place I investigated at was at a pub in Selsey, in Sussex. My friend, Troy, knew the owner's son and he had told Troy about things that had been going on there and he asked him to ask his father if we could investigate there. He was very happy for us to go in and see what we could find. Some of the staff had reported they had seen things out of the corner of their eye, and there was also a local legend that, at some time in the past, a woman had hung herself; it was supposedly around the time of the Second World War.

The pub was quite large and underneath it had two cellars, one quite big and another smaller one. The larger one had supposedly been used as a mortuary for a time during the war. This is where I got very scared for the second time in my life.

On this investigation there were about ten or twelve of us. We split into various groups. In my group there was myself, my then wife, a friend called Stuart and another guy whose nickname was Skelly. The large cellar was quite noisy as the pumps were on and we were all standing at the back. I set the camera on its mount about ten feet in front of us, and slightly to the left of us. It was filming everything else around us too as we all took it in turns to ask out our questions, as we usually did. I had on a very loose-fitting shirt at the time and, on the film, you can see a black shape that looked like a hand poke me in the side! I wasn't worried, more puzzled by it, and I thought, "Bloody hell!" I then moved more into the middle of the group, just to see if anyone else had the same experience. I didn't say why I moved, I just did.

We were still asking out, and at this time I had a person or two each side of me. Suddenly, it felt like someone had shoved a broom handle or something, hard into the small of my back! It was so hard, I had to step forward (with a lot of expletives accompanying it!) and again I had an awful feeling of dread; I can't explain it any better than that, it was awful. I told the group I was with that I had to step outside as I needed a break. No one else had been touched, poked or prodded, only me, so they stayed in the cellar and I went out alone.

I went upstairs and there was someone from the team in the kitchen and another in the smaller cellar, so I knew I was alone. I sat there in the bar for a couple of minutes in the quiet but then I started to hear creaks all round me and I thought, "Oh God, I hate this place." Then the separate teams came back up and it was then time to pack the gear away and call it a night. It was up to me as the one in charge of the camera to go and put it away, and I had to go alone.

By this time, a while had passed since my experience and I was feeling a bit better than I had. I went into the cellar and I said out loud, "If you ever do that to me again, when I die I am going to come back here and find you and beat the shit out of you!" Nothing else happened to me in the cellar after that; another team, not mine, went to investigate and a guy got big scratch marks on him. I have a picture of my oldest son standing where the woman supposedly hung herself, and there are quite a number of orbs and other light anomalies around him, and they are very distinct. We also have pictures of other places there with many orbs in them.

I do recall another time I went there, I was with a medium called Emma and we were in the small cellar. As we got there a little late, the other teams were by this time doing their own thing in various parts of the building, so we went to the smaller cellar where it was only she and I and one other. There was a lot of shelving down one side of the room, with old paint pots on it. We started to ask out that if anyone was there, tap five times to let us know. Sure enough we got the right amount of taps in reply! Suddenly there was an almighty WHACK sound; it sounded like someone had thrown a brick at the paint pots. Emma jumped out of her skin (if she was such a good medium and was supposed to be able to see and communicate with spirits, I couldn't see why she should be getting nervous)!

Finally, I recall one investigation that Simon and I got to do. We had a window of one week we were allowed to go there as it was a military camp. That week the only person there was a caretaker. So, Simon and I went there on the Tuesday.

There is a small museum on the camp with everything relating to explosives, and that had had reports of paranormal stuff going on there. It was during the day we went, as we were not allowed there by night. The main centre of the camp was set in a circle with four quadrangles.

There were four of us in total, and we set off to a disused part of the camp. We were recording and, on the tape, when we replayed it, we distinctly hear a very posh male voice saying, "Please come with me." The voice was very polite and sounded nothing like the males in our group. Apart from that we got not a lot else, but that is just a weird one to finish on.

This story is from a lady called Trina Thompson, she has had to go through (and is still going through) a very tough time. This is her story and I'm sure you would agree, she is going to have a few hurdles to get over before her life gets back on track. She is from Idaho and I saw her on Facebook. I wish her well for the future and hope she gets back to full health soon.

I'm kinda nervous. My journey into life began forty-six years ago, but two-and-a-half years ago I got into a really bad A.T.V accident and it wiped my memory. So, I don't remember anything about my childhood or all the years leading up to my accident. What I do know is the last two-and-a-half years have been interesting, to say the least.

It's very scary to wake up and not know where you're at or who the people are in the room. I remember lying in my hospital bed and there were five of my closest people in the room with me.

I was listening to them talk and while they were talking about the long road that's ahead of me, I began to feel even shittier about my situation than I already did.

At this point I think it was my first full day of being awake. When the accident happened, I was in and out of it for three days. My brain was swelling and I had bleeding as well. While lying there listening to the ladies talk, I was within myself, yelling; yelling at God, at myself, at anyone who would hear me without me speaking. I was angry that I had lived knowing it was gonna be tough on myself and others. I was feeling a tremendous amount of guilt. I felt like I was gonna be more trouble than I was worth. So I was angry at God for not taking me. And while lying there sharing my thoughts to God, a lady appeared in my room; she stood just inside the doorway against the wall. And she began to speak to me; she let me know that I couldn't go, that it wasn't my time, that I still had things to do here, but not to worry, she would be with me from time to time guiding and helping me through my mess. The whole time she's talking I'm wondering why the five ladies sitting next to me aren't hearing or seeing the lady. I remember one of the girls saying something along the lines of, "What is she staring at? Is she seeing something we can't?" The whole time I'm lying there mesmerized by what I'm seeing and hearing and I can't bring myself to speak up.

I spent ten days in the hospital, then another month and a half at a rehab centre learning how to do everything we take for granted again. My first day there I was sharing a room with an elderly lady whom was very loud, so no sleep; thank God my sister was with me.

While I was trying to get situated in my new place, a shadow appeared in my doorway. It was a big, huge, black mass and it kept trying to convince me to come with it. It motioned that if I came with it I would be pain-free; I would be able to walk with no problems; no more seizures or headaches; and, most importantly, I wouldn't be a bother to my family or friends. It scared the crap out of me, unlike the other figure at the hospital. My sister recognized immediately that something was scaring me just by the way I was. I was able to quickly pull my jacked-up legs into my chest. Upon seeing this, the very next day, I got my own room and my childhood friend brought me in several angel figures that she had blessed.

It wasn't until I came home from the hospital that I learned who had visited me in the hospital. I was home a day or two and I had gone into our spare bedroom and on a bookshelf was a picture of a lady; and I knew that's who I'd seen in the hospital. I had no idea it was my late older sister, who had died several years ago from cancer.

To this day I have no clue who or what, the black mass/shadow was in the rehab centre. While in the rehab centre I could lie in bed at night and hear the cries and screams of those since passed; them crying to be let out. They just wanted to go home. Or, the one that stands out the most: "please don't hurt me". No one else could hear these cries because I made sure to ask. For the longest time I thought maybe I was just losing my mind, or it was caused by all the medications I was taking. That is until I came home.

At the time we had roommates who occupied our basement. I was hearing some loud banging one day and proceeded to ask the roommate via text what she was doing, and she responded, "I'm at work no one should be home but you". I was scared and nervous. So, that evening we spoke and she proceeded to tell me about all sorts of things that happen here. And she told me that I've always been able to see and hear and feel things for as long as she's known me, which was about fifteen years or so. I then learned from my sister and others that it was true. I learned that the houses I grew up in were haunted and that almost everywhere I've lived, I've been bothered by noises and seeing things.

My roommate told me that I had seen a Wiccan and a medium and that they both told me similar things about myself, which was I've lived before this life in fact two other times. One during the time of the Salem witch trials and another time being during the trail of tears. I was supposedly burned at the stake during the witch trials and I supposedly walked the trail of tears. They both told me I'm what they call an empath, meaning I can see, feel, and hear things most people do not. Since my accident, all of those abilities have been heightened. I no longer know how to tune it out. So that is something I'm slowly working on. I stay home a lot because of it. I feel most comfortable and safe at home or in the mountains. I don't like a bunch of crowds. I prefer family, or five or so close people or to be alone. I have had to learn who everyone is again.

This is from Melissa of Washington State Paranormal; she has sent this and is again from social media sites.

Sorry it took so long. I don't know where to begin or which story to tell. I feel like this one that is screaming right now is the one I am supposed to tell you. I don't know if you want names or not, but I did ask and they don't mind.

It was a warm summer night in July 2016. The team and I went into Bayview Cemetery to get some evidence. Lisa and Kyle don't know the witches tomb or the location; which I did from a previous public investigation.

As we walked around the outside of Bayview near the woods, we felt like we were being followed. I took my full spectrum camera and started snapping pictures. As the feeling went away, I reviewed the pictures and it started out faint and got stronger and darker; three separate manifestations (I really wish I had my digital recorder going at that time).

We kept walking and we kept seeing shadow people running from tomb to tomb or tree to tomb. Then the smell of food, but of course we are in the Israelite part of the cemetery. Our main focus was the deathbed and the witch's tomb, so we kept walking.

Every once in a while, we see a dash of a shadow person here and there. Once we get to the deathbed, we set up the digital recorder for an EVP (electronic voice phenomenon) session and take some photos. I noticed every time I came here to this spot, there is a shadow figure that is always trying to lure us away.

OK, so, depending on who is around depends on the feeling you get. The first time I was here, the feeling was anger and hatred. But the last two times it has been calm and sadness and lonely. Tonight it seems kind of quiet, so we continue to the witch's tomb. She was quite as active tonight like usually when I come to visit her.

On an EVP I got "all I hear is music" clear as day. A faint scream and old music; not sure what generation but it is old. Then with my own ears I heard, "Can you help me?" I answered it. I have that on EVP. Then the feeling changed to where it was time to go. Something happened to Lisa; she got scratched on her chest.

So, we left, for the safety of the crew. Next day I had to go to cleanse Lisa of the attachment, because she was not herself, or did not feel like herself. We still go in there from time to time and I say ninety per cent of the time we come back with some kind of evidence or experience.

A very short one! This is from Aaron Potter. Found this guy on Facebook. It goes to show that not every story has to be a lengthy one to make a lasting impression on someone.

So – it all started when I was about two to three years old. I was at my uncle's house standing on the staircase. My aunt's house used to be a funeral home. So, I was on the staircase with my uncle (not sure what direction we were heading), I happened to look up and saw this older gentleman at the top of the stairs in front of the stained glass window.

I asked my uncle who that older gentleman was. He looked up and didn't see anybody. He asked, "What gentleman, Aaron?" I said, "That older man up there," as I pointed. Still he didn't see anyone.

That was my first paranormal experience as a child. I would never have known this had my aunt never told me.

These fascinating stories are from a lady from Nova Scotia, her name is Cindy and she belongs to Soul Guidance Paranormal. I think she is a great writer and has had some very strange experiences and has told them here for us. I must say that Canada seems to be a big contributor to this book.

It was the day after my sixth birthday, when we received the news that my paternal grandfather had passed away from the cancer he had been battling. I remember being told he had died, and running out into our yard, behind his house, sobbing. I was very close to him, and would sit by his feet and colour while he watched the news, and spend time with him outdoors in his garden and doing yard work. He and my grandmother lived on the same plot of land. Although he was a strict man, my grandfather had permitted my father to build our home on his land. So, as a young child, I spent a lot of time over at their house.

On that day, when we had received the news of my

83

grandfather's passing, something strange had happened. I remember my father and his brother trying to open my grandfather's tool shed, in the back of his house. But the door had somehow been locked from the inside. There was a little hook lock on the inside of the door. Once they had finally gotten it open, they tried over and over to slam the door different ways, but could not get it to lock from the inside again. They joked that their dad didn't want anyone in around his tools. But their expressions were what stuck with me all these years. They were genuinely perplexed.

My grandmother passed away the very next year, on her husband's birthday. As sad as we were to lose her, we said it was her birthday gift to him, to go and be with my grandfather forever.

Their house stood empty for many years. One day, when I was about fourteen years old, I decided to go inside, to search for an old pair of wooden crutches my grandfather had stored away in the rafters of the basement. My best friend and I entered through the back door, and closed it behind us. It was eerily silent as we crept across the kitchen, opened the basement door, and went down the stairs. We looked around for a few minutes, just being nosey kids. Then, out of nowhere, the basement door at the top of the stairs slammed shut with such force, the whole house shook. It sent us both running as fast as we could up those stairs, across the kitchen, through the small back porch, and flying out the back door. My slightly sore ankle was completely forgotten.

There was not a breath of wind that day. Plus all doors and windows were shut in the house. We could not explain how that door slammed so hard. I truly believe that my grandfather wanted us out of his basement, and he slammed that door to make his point. I will never forget that day.

When something you cannot explain happens to you, each detail seems to get burned into your memory forever.

I can still remember the stale smell of the kitchen, the dank, dark basement, and that feeling of terror as we raced out of the house.

These next few are from Cindy too.

A couple of years later, as I lay awake in my bed in my basement bedroom, I heard footsteps coming down the basement stairs. This was not unusual, as we had a coal furnace, in a room just outside my bedroom, and my father would come down periodically through the night to keep it going. I listened as he walked to the furnace room and waited for him to turn on the light. My room was right at the bottom of the stairs, so I woke up frequently to this light. Not this time. I waited and waited, but the light didn't come on.

I got up from my bed, confused, thinking maybe my dad wasn't ok, but there was no one there. No one had come downstairs at all. I remember that confused, sinking feeling I had; and I am certain of what I heard that night. Those footsteps were so clear and I was wide awake. I sometimes think it was my grandfather, coming to check the furnace for my dad.

My father's brother, whom he was very close to, passed away in his forties, one month before I gave birth to my first child, a daughter, when I was only seventeen. He had been living in Ontario, but when it came close to his time of passing, he was transferred to a hospital close to our family in Cape Breton, Nova Scotia. He ended up passing away in his hospital room only a few short weeks after he was brought home.

A couple of weeks after my daughter was born I was rushed to the hospital, with a very high fever. I remember feeling so cold, I could not stop shaking. It turned out I had a pretty bad infection, and I had to spend a few days, including my first Mother's Day, in the hospital. I ended up staying in the same room my uncle had died in just a few weeks before.

I was lying in the hospital bed one night, falling in and out of sleep having mostly recovered from the fever, when I rolled over and noticed a man sitting on the foot of my bed. I kept my legs tucked up so I wouldn't kick him and I began to talk to him, mid-sentence, as if we were quite familiar and had already been in the middle of a conversation.

I found it strange that he kept his head turned away from me and I couldn't see his face. I turned for a second to look at my bedside clock, and was surprised to see that it was after three am. When I turned back to express this to the man on the bottom of my bed, he had vanished. Confused and a little frightened, I rolled over and, after what seemed like forever, drifted back to sleep. The next morning the realization crept in that what I had experienced was something out of the ordinary. I knew for certain it had not been a dream.

After all these years I will never forget that weight on my bed; how real he felt, and how familiar. I believe in my heart that it was my uncle who came for one last visit.

In my early thirties I began working in a government-owned building, as a cleaner. This building is located in an area of Halifax which would be near the site affected by the Halifax explosion, which happened on December 6th 1917, and took the lives of almost two thousand people. Two ships carrying ammunition collided in the harbour resulting in a massive explosion.

During the first year working there my shift started at 6 am. I was responsible for cleaning a number of offices and classrooms, among other duties.

One morning I walked down the hallway, pushing my cleaning cart. It was almost 6:30 am and I was listening to the radio in my ear buds. From the corner of my eye I saw something bright white, about the size of my palm. It flew down the hallway and passed just above my head on my right. It flew in a spiral motion all the way to the end of the hall, and then disappeared.

My first thoughts were, "That's a huge moth!" Then I realized I would have to pick up that moth, because at the end of the hallway was a closed door. There was nowhere for that large white insect to go. Dreading the thought of touching this thing, I walked to the end of the hall. I searched but found nothing. It was at that point I realized what I had seen was not a moth at all. There was nowhere for it to have gone. I was very perplexed.

Still I didn't think anything paranormal was happening, just something really strange. I hadn't even heard of the term "orb" yet, and I wouldn't tell anyone what I had seen. I thought no one would believe me because if someone had told the same story to me, I would probably have dismissed it as their imagination, or questioned their sanity.

If anyone had asked me up until that point, I did not believe in ghosts. Yet I had clearly seen something out of the ordinary which I could not explain. A few weeks later I had another experience, in that same hallway.

I had been pushing the cleaning cart up the hallway, listening to music, looking down at my feet as I walked. As I passed the doorway to the teleconference room a silver ball, about the size of a marble, rolled out, crossed in front of my feet and disappeared when it hit a row of lockers on the other side of the hall.

It startled me and I looked for the silver ball. It was nowhere to be seen. I looked to the doorway it came from, and realized there was no way it could have come from under that door. It has a door sweep installed, and was tight to the floor. I couldn't even fit my fingers under. The lockers on the other side of the hall, where this silver ball landed, were also all the way to the floor, with no space for anything to go under. Puzzled, I started to realize that something funny was going on, that I didn't quite understand.

About a month later I had walked into that same room,

to vacuum. Immediately upon entering I felt what I can only describe as a feeling of cold hatred, coming from one corner of the room. I tried to ignore what I was feeling, but I felt threatened. Every inch of my body was screaming at me to get out, fast. I quickly left and didn't enter that room again for another two weeks, because of the fear I had felt. I made sure I had a security guard with me, even though I felt silly asking him to come down. It had felt that real to me. The next time I entered, the room felt fine. I never felt that entity in that space again although I always had my guard up when I had to be in that room.

At that point I had approached my co-workers, and asked them if there was something about the building that they weren't telling me. They laughed at me, and one even said, "You're sensitive to something you don't believe in." I had no idea at the time how accurate that statement would turn out to be.

On another occasion, in a room just two doors down, I had entered to clean. As I stepped through the door way I saw a drop of water fall in front of my face. I flinched backward and looked up, but the ceiling was dry. I had this happen in doorways in certain rooms of this building on several occasions. Silvery-looking drops of water would fall close to my face, making me flinch and check for wet spots. On one particular day, the whole ceiling looked as if it were raining water down onto the carpet and desks, for just a few seconds. I had never seen anything like it ever in my life. The entire room was dry, despite the silvery drops I had just seen fall.

I was shocked, and entertained the idea that I might just be crazy after all. I had just seen it raining inside the building.

This building where I worked has only had one recorded death of an employee; an old commissionaire had a heart attack and died during his shift. Many security guards though the years have reported hearing the jingle of keys, and having their names called as they do their rounds.

The land this particular building where I worked is situated on would not only have been near the Halifax explosion site, but is also the location of an old prison, Rockhead Prison, which was torn down many years ago. It is also located very near the Halifax harbour, which is a large body of dirty, flowing water, which happens to be a great conductor of electromagnetic energy. I have measured the electromagnetic frequency with my K2 meter out in the back parking lot, and the energy is off the charts, even out there where there should be no readings at all. The energy inside is even more intense, and it served not only to scare me, but also to wake me up to what was really going on all around us.

After a couple of years working there, my shifts began at 2pm and lasted until 10pm. It was during the evening hours, once everyone had gone home for the day, that I began experiencing more and more activity. Being alone in large sections of the building for hours at a time I listened to music constantly. I was trying to keep my mind off the feeling that I was being watched.

One of my sections was a long hallway, located in an attached "sprung" building. It was a row of offices on one side, with a kitchen at the end. I would unlock, clean, and then lock the offices again, one at a time. On this particular evening I had finished the offices and had pulled my cart into the doorway of the kitchen, backing it in so I could fill it with garbage and access what I needed. As I dumped the first garbage can into my cart, I was looking out into the hallway, pretty relaxed. Out of nowhere the door to one of the offices opened, and slammed hard, right in front of my face. I froze. The lights inside did not come on. I had just been in there, and knew I locked that door. With a sinking feeling in my stomach, I immediately called security. The guard raced down to find me quite panicked, and the door still locked. No one was inside the office or the sprung building, except the guard and me.

As scary as that was I still had to work there, and so I chose to put it out of my mind. For six years. Each time something creepy would happen I would explain it away, as wind, my mind, or anything other than the paranormal.

A few years later, I was given a section in the heart of the building that I was responsible to clean. It was mainly offices in secure parts of the building, which require a key fob to enter.

I had always felt very uneasy in these sections. I tried to get my work done before 8 pm because I was too afraid to be alone in there at night. Sometimes lights would turn on or off, without explanation. I would hear voices, harsh whispers close to my ear, and see shadows out of the corner of my vision. It had a very oppressive atmosphere even though all the people who worked there were very nice.

One afternoon during my shift, I was heading down the hallway to one of the locked areas. At the end of the hall was a cordless vacuum cleaner, sitting with its wand propped up against the glass window. As I started down the hallway, a dark grey ball, about the size of a melon, came around the corner and cut right in front of my abdomen, causing me to jump back. I watched it zig zag down the hallway, bouncing off each side wall and, when it hit the end, it knocked over the vacuum cleaner wand before it disappeared around a corner. I couldn't believe my eyes. It was so shocking and out of the boundaries of what I believed in. I will never forget exactly what I saw and felt that day; every detail of that experience seems to be burned into my memory.

One quiet evening I was alone, vacuuming an office in my area. I had my music going, trying to ignore the creepy feelings I was having. I was dancing and singing along to Rod Stewart's "Do ya think I'm Sexy". When I sang the part "just reach out and touch me ..." I felt a strong tap in the small of my back.

I turned, expecting a co-worker, only to find I was

alone. Confused, I checked to see if I had accidentally bumped something but there was nothing near my back. I looked at the position of the vacuum hose, which was not anywhere near my back either. Ignoring my instincts I went back to vacuuming, quietly singing, very on edge. I felt another tap, same spot. That was enough for me. I packed up the vacuum, and went running out the main doors. I felt foolish but terrified at the same time. I couldn't continue on like this. I needed to find out what was happening.

On a recent trip toward an investigation, we were heading from Prince Edward Island, to Cape Breton Island. It was about 9 pm, and it was pretty dark as we drove the winding road through St. Peter's, on our way to Sydney. I was in the passenger seat watching the road, a little nervous because it was known as a dangerous stretch of road with many twists and dark, dangerous curves. I was tired from the day's investigating, trying to relax, but alert.

Suddenly, about thirty feet in front of our car, in the middle of the road, I saw legs. A dark black torso and a set of legs, the size of a large man, quickly ran across the road. The apparition was much darker than the surroundings and, when it hit the far side of the road, I could no longer see it. I sat up quickly in my seat, astonished at what I had just seen. I had never seen a shadow person before and, even though it was only the lower half, I was both shocked and excited. For two days it was all I could think of. The image of the legs running across the road played over and over in my mind.

If I had been driving when I saw the legs I would have probably slammed on the brakes, as an immediate reaction to seeing a person in the road. I wondered if maybe this apparition had anything to do with the many accidents on this stretch of road.

Cindy has also sent this. I find it sad and have never had a story told like this one before.

I was not sure whether to include this one, but I figured I will. I channelled a story one day from one of the child spirits that lives here in our home with us. It is her story. I just picked up a pen one day, and out it came. It was the story of how we met Mary, the little girl who we still have here in our home. The response on YouTube has been very positive. I made a little video of it where I narrate her story myself. It was a very surreal experience to sit and have an entire story flow from the tip of my pen, with no thought involved, no corrections, not even a spelling error. It just flowed. Anyway, here it is.

Mary's story

I have a story I would like to share with you. It came to me one day, while I was reviewing evidence that was totally unrelated to this matter. I felt the need to pick up a pen and paper, and the rest just flowed. I had no plans on writing anything that day, or any other day. I felt no need, or right to edit what I had written.

Mary was a lonely little girl. She played each day by herself; wandering around, trying to find someone, anyone, to notice her, to listen.

Things in Mary's world had been grey and foggy for a long time. She remembers playing with her stuffed bear on the floor of her bright and sunny room. There was a window seat next to her, with lots of fat, squishy pillows. Many afternoons she played, and napped, in that very seat. She remembers pretending to be a princess, and tea parties with her bear, while wearing her pretty, long white nightgown. Or maybe, all these things existed only in her mind.

In reality she felt all dirty, and ragged, hungry and alone. She longed for the feel of a loving embrace; caring arms to hold her. But feelings like that were distant. They were a distant memory for Mary.

She was six, with light brown, mid-back length, straight hair. She was the perfect size for her age, but slim. She had dark circles around her eyes, and was very pale.

Mary vaguely remembers finding a little girl in her room one day. Mary had just woken up and there she was, on the floor of Mary's room. She looked just like Mary.

"How can this be?" wondered Mary, beginning to panic. She raced downstairs to tell someone to get some help. She was so confused. The house seemed empty. No Mama, or Dad; no housekeeper. Where had they all gone?

Sad, scared, confused Mary slowly climbed the large wooden staircase, back upstairs. Surely Mom would be in her room.

A frantic search brought Mary back to the door of her own bedroom. She stared at the closed door. "Maybe it's all a dream," she thinks. Slowly her little hand reaches for the doorknob, to take a peek at what waits on the other side.

Her hand slips, and goes right through the knob. She tries again, and again. Mary can hardly believe her eyes. She holds out her tiny hands, flipping them over, examining the palms and the backs, over and over; trying to make sense of what was happening.

She tries again for the doorknob just to be sure, and her hand passes through it again. Surely, she is dreaming, she reasons, in her six-year-old mind. She reaches up to knock on the door, and her hand passes right through that too. Giggling a little, at this 'dream super power', the little girl steps through the door and back into her bedroom.

It's empty. No little girl that looked just like her on the floor anymore. Great, it must have been another part of her dream, she thinks. Mary sits down, and picks up her favourite bear. He is pretty solid to her. And so she begins to play tea party, setting her bear up in a chair, and taking her place at the small table across from him.

She doesn't notice time pass; playing, occasionally

wondering when everyone would return to the house. She thought it was strange for a very long time, that she would be left all alone like this. But, being a good little girl, Mary plays in her room, never making a fuss, waiting for someone, any one of her family members to return home, to find her waiting.

After what seemed like an eternity to the small girl, she heard a noise downstairs. Someone was finally home. She rushed down the stairs, only to find two strangers in the house. She's worried, and hides at first; watching them from a distance, clutching her bear.

"Why are they here? How did they get in? "she wonders. Eventually, curiosity gets the best of the little girl and she approaches the couple. They seem like nice people, and they are carrying some funny tools.

"Hello," Mary says, but they don't respond. They don't even look at her. "Hey!" she shouts, as loud as she can. Still she got no response. Frustrated, Mary stands in front of the lady, who has a strange little black box with lights in her hand.

"Hi," says Mary. The lady starts to talk. She tells Mary that her name is Cindy, and the man with her, who was walking around, looking at all the things in the house, was Jeremie. The lady keeps talking, and mentions something about the date. That didn't mean a whole lot to a six-year-old. Mary just knows she has been alone a long time, and maybe these people can help her find her mom, and the rest of her family who so strangely disappeared.

Excited, Mary jumps up and down and tries to tug at the lady's sleeve. The lights on the little box the lady is carrying, light up. "Meter hit," says Cindy. "We may have something here." Cindy starts to explain that if someone just touched the meter, that it just measures their energy, and asked if they could touch it again.

"Why can't she see me, or hear me? She's talking to me, I think." Mary touches the meter again. It lights up. Fun! Mary starts to forget about her bedroom, her bear, her little table and chairs; and she became fixated on this kind lady, with the funny tools.

She follows the couple around her house, beginning to notice that some things in her house were now broken; some windows, cupboards, and the floor seemed a little off, on a slant. "What was happening? Why does everything look so different? Where are my parents? Is this really a dream? "

Fear and confusion flood in, and as the couple get ready to leave the house, Mary realizes she will be left alone again. Even though the lady said that no one was allowed to follow them, Mary clings. She clings to hope. She clings to comfort. She clings to this couple; attached, now to the only comfort she can find.

She never quite understood what this 'light' is, that Cindy was telling her to look for. Waiting; still hoping to one day be reunited with her long-lost family.

Although this story was written by me, I do not feel as if it is my story. It belongs to that sweet, lonely little girl, who I still hear each night. Her giggles and pleas for help, captured on the audio I record in my bedroom, as she plays and fights with the other little ones, who have made our home their new home.

This story also brings our attention to the fact that most parents in Western culture do not teach their children about death. No one wants to bring up such a serious subject with a child, who may or may not even understand what we are talking about. In my opinion, this results in the many child spirits that I encounter when I am on investigations. The greatest number, in my experience, seem to be in old military forts, dating back to the late 1800s to early 1900s; although I have found a few in abandoned homes and cemeteries.

These child spirits, for the most part, have no idea that they have died. Through audio recordings, I have found that many of the parents and other adults, who are around these young ghosts, are actively trying to hide their true condition from the children.

Some of these adults may not even understand that they are deceased. They may not have been religious, and most did not believe in an afterlife, and they certainly did not believe in ghosts. They seem to carry on, though, in a life constructed like a daydream, with no concept of time and no end in sight.

I wanted to share another story. It happened at Fairview Cemetery, in Halifax, which is also the site of some of the *Titanic* graves as well. It is a huge cemetery located next to the end of the Bedford Highway, at the Windsor Street Exchange. It is an extremely active cemetery. Not all good energies, either. I have the story already written and the actual video of the experience as well. It was Jeremie's first time ever having a paranormal experience. It was the case that ignited our passion for helping lost souls. When I speak of "work", it is the same haunted building I describe in the previous stories.

One day I walked into work, after being off for a while, I was wearing a raincoat. As I walked up one of the ramps in the building, something grabbed the back bottom of my coat, tugging up, down, up, down. Startled I yelled out, "Don't do that!" I turned around quickly, only to see that I was alone on the ramp. I believe it was one of the child spirits trying to get my attention, because of how low my coat was grabbed. It would have to be someone short. Afterward I felt bad for yelling, and a little embarrassed. I was sure the child meant no harm, and I probably scared him as much as he scared me.

Eventually I bought a K2 meter, which measures electromagnetic frequency, or EMF. Basically, it's a power meter with lights to indicate when it detects power, or electricity. It is thought that spirit energy can interact with these meters, by touching or coming close to it, and lighting up the lights. It can be used as a communication tool with the spirit lighting up the lights for 'yes' answers, or leaving it dark, for 'no' answers.

A few months into this paranormal experimentation, I had a strong feeling that I needed to go to a nearby graveyard. I passed this cemetery every day on my way to work, and had never given it a second thought. I put it off but, each day, the thought would creep back into my mind that I needed to go there. I tried to arrange for a co-worker to accompany me, but it never seemed to work out.

One night the feeling was so strong; I called my best friend and convinced him to meet me there after work. We walked around the cemetery for about thirty minutes, trying to get someone to interact with us. Just as we were about to give up, our meter lit up. I asked if someone was there, could they light it up again, and they did. It lit up all the lights. I explained how the meter works and how we could use it as a yes/no tool.

Question after question, the meter lit up on command. Through these perfectly timed responses, we learned that we were talking to a teenage boy. He was very confused. He told us that he had not been there very long. His family was still living nearby. He had a mother, father, and an older brother. He didn't know what had happened. When I explained to him that he no longer had his physical body, that he had died, the meter went very quiet.

I apologized for upsetting him, and the meter lit up. I told this young man that it was OK for him to go into the light now. I asked him if he could see angels around me, and the meter lit up, indicating a yes answer. I was floored. He could see them around us. This was amazing to me, and very humbling, as I was still quite shaky in my faith.

Once I convinced the young man he would still be able to check in on his parents after he went to the light, the meter went crazy. I told him he could ask the angels around us to show him the way home. After that, the meter went silent. Not a single light lit up as we made our way out of the graveyard. He was gone.

We were elated as we left the cemetery. Neither of us had expected any activity. We certainly didn't expect an entire conversation with a deceased young man. That night ignited a passion in me, and I knew I had found what I was meant to be doing. I have never gotten another urge to return to that place, yet.

I found this group on Twitter, seeing their name I thought they were from Scotland, which was good as I had no stories from there. Then I looked closer and they are from Virginia, USA! Well, here is the story that was sent in for you.

My name is Jacob Fife, and I have been a paranormal investigator for about nine years now and I have seen a lot of scary things, but nothing like what I saw in a sanatorium I investigated.

It was during a public event, and my dad and I were with a group that was investigating a second floor hallway that was once a part of the children's ward of the sanatorium. I had investigated the building a few times before and so we decided to split off from the group to go check out this one room that is known to be extremely active.

We made it to this room where a person had been killed violently and there were two others with us and we started a spirit box session. We started getting a few voices over the box, but our attention was drawn to movement and noises coming from the hallway. We kept seeing large shadow figures and hearing stuff being moved around in the room across from us, but when we'd check there would be no one there. We decided to turn off the spirit box to see what we could hear with our own ears, and the room quickly got this very dark and evil feeling to it, and we all could feel a very dark presence near us.

I asked for the spirits to make a sound and we heard a

deep, guttural growl come from inside the room we were in! We all jumped back a bit and, when I later checked our voice recorder, the growl was not recorded somehow. After a while it felt like whatever entity was near kept getting closer and finally it was like all hell broke loose. It sounded like objects were being thrown, glass shattering, and people stomping in the room across from us, but no one was there and nothing had been moved.

About this time our guide came in the room and he said that everyone had been looking for us, and that we had pretty much disappeared, and no one heard us or any of the other noises. The last thing I remember is I was walking out of the room talking with the guide and then all of a sudden my dad and I were in a completely different room. I don't remember how we got there, I don't remember walking there; but we were in this room in the back corner of a hallway.

After about a minute I saw movement by the door and, when I looked, I saw this creature standing in the door. It was about seven feet tall, was shaped almost like a giant blob, and it was pitch black. It was standing in the doorway and then it ran back towards the hallway, and for some reason I chased it. I chased it into the hallway and then it stopped and turned to face me head on. I stopped dead in my tracks about three feet away from this thing and we made eye contact. It was huge, and it had a crooked smile and large black eyes, and it had this very warm heat coming off of it that made me sweaty.

About this time, my dad ran into the hallway and he told me to back away slowly. We backed up back into the room we were in originally, and we conducted a short spirit box session to try and speak with it. It did speak to us, and it had a very scratchy and metallic voice, but none of it was recorded on our voice recorder when I went back and reviewed it.

After a few minutes we felt like it was in our best interests to leave and, as we left, we could see this creature walking towards us and it looked like it had long arms outstretched towards us. I've been back there twice since that experience and I haven't seen anything like that ever again.

I contacted HBI (Haunted Britain Investigations) through Twitter. They are a prolific team and do many investigations, which in every case they post on YouTube. They have this story documented on there too if you would like to go on and see for yourself.

HBI Haunted Britain Investigations are a very respected paranormal team in the United Kingdom.

Over the years, HBI have had the privilege to investigate some of Britain's most haunted buildings, including historic castles, theatres, prisons and inns. We use specialist equipment to try and document the paranormal claims of each location. One particular location, Ye Olde Trip to Jerusalem Inn is an historic pub in Nottingham and has certainly lived up to its reputation as one of the oldest and most haunted inns in England.

Built into the sandstone rock, this inn sits directly below Nottingham castle. The cellar is caves that now house the ale barrels, and is home to a condemned man's cell, originally from the castle above.

In the rock room, encased in glass and covered in decades of dust, is the cursed galleon. It is thought to be cursed because the last few people who cleaned the galleon died unexpectedly within weeks of doing so. This is the reason why it now resides in a glass case covered in thick black dust.

There are many paranormal claims at the Inn, from: a haunted snug; a World War Two airman that has been seen standing at the lounge fireplace; a young girl who plays upon the stairs; and, a famous landlord of the Inn from the late 1800s nicknamed "Yorkie". He is said to appear in the vast cave cellars and makes himself known by shouting and throwing tankards. With all these claims, HBI had to investigate.

The team, run by Gemma and Lee Davies, have investigated the Inn nine times and during those nine investigations the team have caught some jaw-dropping evidence.

Lee and a fellow team member were setting up motion detectors in the cellar caves and decided to leave an audio recorder in the condemned man's cell. They left it recording and carried on setting up the equipment. Upon analysis of the recording they were shocked to hear a loud male voice cry out, "Help, please!" over the top of the team members. This disembodied voice wasn't heard at the time! Could this be some kind of residual energy from the past, or the lost soul of a condemned man calling out for help?

On another investigation, the HBI team decided to set up a locked off camera in the rock room of the Inn. We left the camera running for most of the night until the investigation was over. When watching the footage back the team again were shocked to hear loud footsteps run up the stairs and into the room, only for the camera to not show any physical persons present at the time. With all members of the team accounted for, this too remains unexplained.

In this same area, on a previous investigation, Lee was sitting at a table when he stood up in shock and told the team that something had just blown in his face. The team replied that they hadn't heard or seen anything near Lee at that moment, but Lee's digital audio device placed on the table had caught what sounds like something hissing or spitting at Lee seconds before he reacts. Again, this remains unexplained.

HBI Haunted Britain Investigations have caught numerous EVP (electronic voice phenomena) during their investigations at the Inn. These include intelligent responses to questions asked. One, in the haunted snug, thought to be the airman. One team member asked, "Are you still here?" On the team's SB7 device that creates white noise through radio frequencies, they got the response, "Yes... I'm still here". Another team member asked, "Are you with us? Come on sweetie," only to get an EVP back saying, "I'm no sweetie."

Recently, in the cellar caves, we think we might have finally made contact with past landlord "Yorkie". Gemma and Steve, who is the team medium, were holding a vigil using a REM-Pod device. This device emits an electromagnetic field that surrounds the device; if the field is broken it alarms and lights up. Steve picked up on a gentleman spirit wearing a leather apron and asks for him to come forward. He says that the gentleman is laughing. Gemma asks questions and after each question the REM-Pod alarms then stops. To make sure it is the spirit of the man, she asks for it to make the REM-Pod alarm stronger and louder; it does so immediately. Gemma then suspects that this is the Inn's famous landlord "Yorkie". She calls his name and asks if it's him, the REM-Pod alarms again straight away then stops. With no interference or contamination, and baseline readings of that area on zero Miligaus, this too remains unexplained.

These are just some of the strange and unexplained experiences HBI have managed to document at this ancient historic pub in the heart of Nottingham. You can see all this footage, and hear the EVPs, at HBI Haunted Britain Investigations YouTube channel, and, if you ever find yourself in Nottingham, England, go and enjoy some ale at Ye Olde Trip to Jerusalem Inn ... just don't ask for the spirits!

These next stories are sent as case notes, which for me shows the different ways people record and store things. I hope you like the way they have sent them; I think it is nice to see something set out in such a different style. They are from Virginia and again found on the Interweb! They assure me that those who are named in these stories are good with that. Rodney is the person who sent them.

Black Diamond Paranormal
<u>Final Report and Analysis</u>
Case 004

Historical Pocahontas Cemetery, September 20, 2008, Pocahontas, Virginia

Investigators
Rodney Shortridge, Robyn Belcher, Teresa Dillon, John Belcher, Aaron Shortridge & Allen Gross

On September 20th 2008 the BDPS team investigated the Historical Pocahontas Cemetery located at Pocahontas, Virginia. All of the BDPS team members did an outstanding job with such a huge area to investigate. I would like to personally thank the Mayor of Pocahontas, Anita Brown, for giving BDPS permission to investigate the cemetery. With the help of councilwoman Amy Flick, along with the President of the Historical Society Tom Childress, we were able to obtain a lot of history and knowledge of the historical importance of this cemetery. We started around 2:30 pm and did our investigation until 12:30 am. Around 8:00 pm we were joined by councilwoman Amy Flick and Rachel, the Exhibition Mine Curator, on our investigation.

Equipment used at this site included (4) DVRs, (3) microcassette recorders, (2) camcorders, (1) laser thermometer, (1) K2 meter and (4) digital cameras. As we do in our investigations, we place the DVRs in areas that were reported to have high paranormal activity. The camcorders were placed to get the best view of the cemetery and the microcassette recorders were held by my son, Aaron; Teresa; and Allen while we were doing our EVPs.

While conducting our investigations, a few of the team members and I had personal paranormal experiences.

Aaron experienced having strong feelings of being watched although no one was in the area; hearing a knocking sound coming from inside one of the tombs; and seeing a white figure duck down behind a headstone. This event was also witnessed by Robyn. When they went to the head stone to investigate there was no evidence of anyone in that area. Aaron also experienced the feeling of someone breathing on his neck, and something tugged on his shirt. He describes it like a child tugging. Aaron and Robyn both describe seeing a bright white orb come up over a headstone and then disappear. Aaron also describes hearing voices. Teamed with Aaron, Robyn experienced her hair being pulled, feeling several cold spots and witnessing a long, white, floating apparition.

Later in the night, Robyn describes the feeling as though something had walked through her. At this time, Allen was close enough to take a picture of the event and the photo clearly shows a mist surrounding Robyn.

Later that night, Aaron and Teresa were teamed together. Teresa experienced seeing a white figure near a tree. As they went to investigate, the figure was no longer there. Aaron also experienced a sharp pain in his back, just below his left shoulder blade. He describes the pain like someone had stuck a knife into his back and the pain lasted for around ten minutes.

My experiences began around 8:00 pm while I was teamed with Teresa. We were walking back up the hill from the old entrance and, to my left in the woods, I heard someone call my name. Teresa was on my right side and the rest of the teams were on top of the hill. When we got up the hill, I asked everyone did they call my name and everyone said no. I feel this was something paranormal because the fact when my name was called, it was like someone speaking in a very low voice, so low that Teresa didn't hear it. Later that night, still teamed with Teresa, we were sitting on the tailgate of the truck. I noticed a very bright, white mist circle around a tree. I got Teresa's attention and she noticed right before it disappeared. As we went to investigate the tree, there were no signs of any more activity.

We were able to obtain a great deal of evidence of paranormal activity in the form of EVPs (electronic voice phenomenon) with one of the DVRs (Digital Voice Recorder) and the microcassette recorders, photos containing orbs, unexplained lights and two apparitions.

The investigation of this historical cemetery was a huge success due to the fact that we got sixty-four EVPs (electronic voice phenomenon). Out of these there are thirty-one that are very clear and loud. That is a very high success rate. We also got photos of various-sized and different coloured orbs; unexplained light phenomena; and, what we have come to the conclusion are, two apparitions.

We heard the following EVPs (electronic voice phenomenon):

1   Young male's voice with foreign accent "Footo"
2   Human voice "Growl"
3   Young child's voice "I push it"; sounded excited
4   Whisper "Oh Rodney"
5   Heavy Breaths
6   Female Voice "Why don't you just come over?"
7   Young female voice "Trying to communicate"
8   Old female voice "Here, what's happen? Uh …"
9   Male voice "Damn it!"
10 Male voice "Wrong way"
11 Female voice "It's them"
12 Male voice "Oh shit"
13 Black female voice "I better go now"

14   Little girl "Mamma, I want to go"
15   A child's voice "Come here!"
16   Little girl "I want it"
17   Little girl "Mamma"
18   Whistling
19   Little girl "Mom"
20   Whistling; same as in 18
21   Whistling; same as in 18 & 20
22   Whistling; same as in 18 & 20 & 21
23   Childs voice "I'm here"
24   Female voice "Please help!"
25   Infant Baby crying
26   Female voice "Walk this way"
27   Male voice "Hey, over here!"; this sounds like a foreign accent, possibly Irish
28   Female voice "Why?"
29   Female voice "Hello"
30   Child laughing
31   Female voice "Yeah"

We have come to the conclusion that this cemetery has a very high rate of paranormal activity in the form of EVPs, orb activity, apparitions and unexplained lights and mists. Our hope is to one day to get permission to investigate this cemetery again with more advanced equipment and more personnel to be able to cover the vastness of this great historical cemetery.

I would like to add, what an honour it is to have been invited to a tremendous historical site in Southwest Virginia. The people who came from all over the world to help build this town are buried here and they deserve to be remembered with dignity. My heart sank when I saw how desecrated so many of the memorials are. I realize this town does not have the funds needed for the vast repairs. Tazewell County, the state of Virginia, and the United States Historical Societies should combine forces to allocate funding to the Pocahontas Cemetery.

The local community and local government could

donate time and supplies to restore the place where so many lie at rest because they gave their lives to build this community. The men, women, and children buried here deserve to have a memorial worthy of their sacrifice. I also believe there should be monument to the miners who were killed during the early days of this town and who are buried in unmarked graves. Their names should be placed for all to read. My suggestion is to start a fund drive asking the public, statewide and worldwide, to donate to the building of a memorial to the miners.

This was our fourth investigation and it was a phenomenal success. I feel very strongly that the Historical Pocahontas Cemetery warrants further investigation to get more evidence of the paranormal that seems to exist there. We have been very fortunate to have captured such great evidence. I feel much honoured to have had the success we had.

BDPS is introducing three new members, they are: John Belcher; Robyn's husband, Shawn Hamlin; and, Allen Gross. One has experience in the technical fields and is also clairvoyant, one is an investigator and consultant, the other is an investigator in training. We look forward to working with these individuals and the experiences and knowledge they have will be an asset to BDPS. Their commitment to helping BDPS in finding evidence to support the existence of the paranormal may allow us to come one step closer to explaining the paranormal phenomenon.

Final Report and Analysis
Case 015
Pocahontas Cemetery Phase I

August 15, 2009, Pocahontas, Virginia

Investigators
Rodney Shortridge, Robyn Belcher, Aaron Shortridge,
Mike Brown, Amy Flick & John Belcher

On August 15th, 2009, the BDPS team investigated the Pocahontas Cemetery located in Tazewell County in the town of Pocahontas, Virginia. I would like to take this moment to thank Amy Flick and Mayor Adam Cannoy for contacting BDPS and giving us permission to investigate such an historical site. We decided to use three teams to investigate this site. The first team consisted of Robyn and me. The second team consisted of Aaron and Amy Flick. The third team consisted of Mike and Johnny. We started our investigation around 8:00 pm and finished around 2:30 am.

Equipment used at this site included (6) DVRs (Digital Voice Recorders), (3) microcassette recorders, (2) camcorders with night vision, (5) digital cameras, (1) K2 meter, (1) EMF meter and (1) laser thermometer along with other devices for experiments. We tried to recreate the set-up as we did in our last investigation of the cemetery, to try and get a response from the child EVPs (electronic voice phenomena) by using toys that light up and that play music. As we try to do in all of our investigations, we placed the DVRs in areas that have reports of paranormal activity or areas of interest. With the knowledge from our last investigation, this helped in the placing of our equipment in hopes of getting evidence. Both night vision camcorders were placed in the top area of the cemetery, facing one another, in attempts to capture any video evidence. The microcassette recorders were held by each team as they investigated the cemetery.

We started the investigation by dividing the cemetery into three grids; one for each team. Team one consisted of me and Robyn. We investigated the right side lower end of the cemetery, covering an area about 75 to 100 yards from the top of the cemetery down to the main road going into Pocahontas. Team two consisted of Mike and Johnny; they investigated the very top section of the cemetery, covering about 100 yards. Team three consisted of Aaron and Amy; they investigated the left side lower end of the cemetery, also covering an area about 100 yards from the top of the cemetery down to the main road going into Pocahontas. Each team worked on a rotation.

About every two hours, each team would rotate to the area of the last team that was investigating. A few times during the investigation we also switched up team members. This was a great experience for the entire team to be investigating such a large area. We decided that the vast area of the cemetery would be best investigated in two phases. Phase one went as to plan; phase two will be conducted in the spring of 2010.

Personal Experiences:
Robyn Belcher:

About forty-five minutes into the investigation, me and Rodney were sitting and talking. During this time a cold hand touched my shoulder. When we made our way to the top of the hill, we were sitting and resting and I heard a female whisper "Rodney". Later, me and Rodney and Aaron took the top centre of the cemetery. Close to the camera farthest down we sat to watch for shadows that several others had seen. After a few minutes we all saw a shadow the size of a child peeking in and out of several headstones and a tree, almost like it was playing with us. At the same time, Aaron had been hearing noises behind us in the road. I caught several blue orbs during him hearing this. A few minutes later I turned to my left and a blue face was right in front of mine, just for a half a second. This was the first time I felt uneasy that night. The second was when Mike and I went back to see if he could see the child shadow playing. At first, we heard what sounded like footsteps in a few isolated areas then, all at once, it was everywhere.

Amy Flick:

At one point Aaron and I kept smelling flowers. Or maybe some kind of cheap perfume! We searched for flowers but didn't find anything that would cause the smell. I did feel like somebody was following me around all night long. Every time I turned around to take a picture I got the same green orb. I did witness the little boy/girl playing hide-and-seek or just watching us from behind the tombstones. Only saw him twice, though. I got cold chills – I do not think from his presence, though, just because it was pretty neat.

Mike Brown:

While investigating the upper area with Johnny, we were talking about the miners and masons that were buried there. While speaking to Johnny, I saw a shadow move from one headstone to behind a tree. Once again, in this area, there was a general creepy feeling. While investigating the location behind the tree, Johnny explained that was the same general area where we captured the "I Push It" EVP.

Rodney Shortridge:

While investigating the lower end of the cemetery with Robyn, I heard my name "Rodney" whispered. I asked Robyn, "Was that you?" and she said "no" and that she heard it too. After rotating and also changing some of the team members with other members, Robyn, Aaron and I were investigating the centre top of the cemetery and we were sitting close to the road. With all the flashlights off, and while Robyn was taking pictures behind us, I saw a shadow when the flash went off. It moved from one headstone to another one. The shadow was short, like a child. I asked Robyn and Aaron to watch in the direction that I saw the shadow and with lights off and no flashing from the cameras. A few minutes passed and then, from behind a tree, the shadow moved to another headstone and then to another one. Robyn and Aaron agreed they saw what I was seeing. I felt a little chill in the air but not much. After watching the shadow move from one headstone to another for about fifteen minutes and asking questions to try to get a response, we investigated the area where the shadow was moving back and forth. We tried to find out what could have been causing this event and we could not find anything to explain what we saw. It is my conclusion this was a shadow of a small child we were seeing. We took pictures of the event and nothing conclusive came of them.

Photo evidence: shows an apparition of a small child sitting between a tree and headstone, where we saw the shadow later that night.

EVPs (Electronic Voice Phenomenon)

We heard the following EVPs (electronic voice phenomenon) and unexplained noises on our DVRs (Digital Voice Recorders) & microcassette recorders:

Unexplained clicks; unexplained Female Laugh; unexplained Laugh; unexplained Whistling.

We have come to the conclusion that the Pocahontas Cemetery still has high paranormal activity. But on this night the activity was very low compared to our previous investigation in September of 2008. This may have been due to the fact that there was a celebration going on in the town of Pocahontas on this night that was less than a mile from the cemetery. We heard the party noises ourselves for several hours. Could this have had an effect on the activity in the cemetery? Possibly; there is no way of testing this theory. We look forward to coming back in the spring of 2010 to investigate this historical site with more advanced equipment. This was our fifteenth investigation and it was a great success. We have been very fortunate to have had the opportunity to be working with such a historical town as Pocahontas, Virginia and with Amy Flick. I feel honoured to have had the success we've had and to be working alongside such a professional team.

I feel honoured to be working with such a great team. Without the team's hard work and professionalism, BDPS would not be what it has become today.

Final Report and Analysis
Case 022

Lake Shawnee Amusement Park, June 18, 2010

Located between Princeton, West Virginia & Spanishburg, West Virginia

Investigators
Rodney Shortridge, Mike Brown, Amy Flick, Matt O'Quin, Heather Lamantia. Special guests: Clayton Trout & Dr. Shari Stacy

On June 18th, 2010 the BDPS team investigated Lake Shawnee Amusement Park, located between Princeton, West Virginia & Spanishburg, West Virginia. I would like to take this moment to thank Mr. Gaylord White for giving us permission to investigate such an interesting site. We decided, because of the size of the park, that each team would investigate separate areas of the park and adjoining property simultaneously, while one member would watch the camera monitor in our base tent (which was previously set up). We started our investigation around 7:00 pm with a walking tour of the park that was given by Mr. White. We started our set up around 9:00 pm then proceeded to our investigation soon after. We finished our investigation around 6:30 am the following morning. Each team worked on a rotation, changing their location about every 3 hours. This was a great experience and very helpful in our constant training.

EQUIPMENT USED AT THIS INVESTIGATION:
- (9) DVR's (Digital Voice Recorders)
- (2) microcassette recorders
- (4) Zero Lux low lever IR (infra-red) cameras
- (2) Kodak digital cameras
- Nikon camera
- Fuji digital camera

- Canon digital camera
- Samsung digital cameras
- Motion diction IR (infra-red) Field video/camera
- K2 meters
- EMF (Electro Magnetic Field) meter
- Laser thermometers

We placed 1 DVR (Digital Voice Recorder) in each of the areas of the park with reports or claims of paranormal activity, including the ticket booth, abandoned mobile home (aka Hot Dog Stand) by the lake, Ferris wheel, chain-link swing set and the upper end of the property away from the park. The 2 IR cameras were placed at the upper end of the property to cover the entire field, 2 microcassette recorders were carried by two different teams. Also, each team carried along with them during their investigations one of the following; K2 meters, EMF (Electro Magnetic Field) meter or laser thermometers.

Reports & claims:
There have been many tragic claims at this location that have allegedly ended in death. The tragic killings of the Clay family members, history shows actually happened. Also, claims have been made about a swing that was once near the ticket booth, which is no longer there: a truck making deliveries to the park accidentally backed up into the path of the swing, and a young girl was killed when she allegedly was struck by the delivery truck. Further claims have been made about a boy drowning in a swimming pool that was on the property many years ago; some Chicago men being killed and buried on the property; people being attacked by unseen and seen spirits and demons; unexplained disembodied voices, orbs, dancing lights, shadows and apparitions, which could be the un-resting spirits of the Clay family or possibly the Natives who once lived on the property. There have been many paranormal investigations conducted on this property throughout the

years, with people coming from around the world and even big TV networks, and it was also featured on ABC's Top 10 Scariest Places TV Show hosted by Linda Blair. A high percentage have come away from their investigations with the conclusion that this property is haunted. The Ferris wheel that is on the property was bought and placed on the property in the 50s and, from our research, no one has died or been killed on this ride. The swings that are near the Ferris wheel have reports of a certain swing moving on its own for no reason and most people have the misconception that this is the swing in which the girl was killed. That assumption is incorrect. The swing that the girl allegedly was accidently killed on is no longer on the property. Also on the property is an old, run-down mobile home that Mr. White said was the hot dog stand. At the time of our investigation the area was badly flooded which made it very difficult to cover the entire park area of the property. The park is now an area for local catfish tournaments, which are held on the site weekly.

Our historian Dave Horn worked many long weeks and hours to find all the history of the Lake Shawnee Amusement Park and these are his findings.

Lake Shawnee: Historical Findings
By Black Diamond Paranormal Society historian, Dave Horn

Black Diamond Paranormal Society (aka BDPS) was given the opportunity to investigate the property in Princeton, W.V., locally known as 'The Lake Shawnee Amusement Park'. BDPS was tasked with recording any potential evidence that was considered 'paranormal'. In addition to the paranormal investigation, BDPS conducted a formal, historical investigation in hopes of understanding possible causes to current-day phenomena. Contained herein are the findings of the historical investigation.

The property has a rich recorded history. Beginning in the late 1700s, documentation begins with the locally known story of the 'Clay Family Massacre'. I have found very little to add to the already researched and well-documented account of the massacre occurring on the park's premises.

The next part of the folklore and legend that surrounds the park is the alleged haunting of a girl, boy and/or children who died due to a mechanical swing malfunction. This is a completely unverifiable story. I have spent days in the library researching old newspaper articles via microfiche and have yet to find any evidence that would give credence to any deaths at the amusement park itself.

I personally verified with the Mercer County Police Department on August 4th, 2010 that there are no recorded cases of children dying or being injured due to any sort of ride-related incident. I also interviewed multiple employees of the County Clerk's office regarding this urban legend. None that I interviewed could recall any stories of that nature ever being spread. None could recall anything regarding a ride malfunction. Two recalled a story of a child drowning in the pool in the 50s, but both added that it may have just been a story. I am inclined to use these testimonies as fact due to those being interviewed, (a) being people between the ages of sixty and seventy-five thus being the appropriate age to have attended the park during the 50s as children/young adults and (b) having lived locally their entire lives. Therefore, giving said testimonies 'first-hand account' credibility. It is my final conclusion that the alleged 'death by swing' story is nothing more than a myth, being created in the proximity of the past twenty years.

In researching the previous deeds of the property, I found very little of interest with the exception of the following. In a deed recorded in Book No. 9 page 496 dated June 1859, the contents of the deed deviated from the regularly formatted legal jargon from previous deeds. The following is the additional wording of the contract:

"An elderly woman currently residing in a cabin upon

the aforementioned grounds shall remain on these grounds and continue to have free use of the dwelling until she meets the end of her natural life. At which time, the current owners of the property shall provide a proper and decent Christian burial for her, where she shall remain forever."

Simply stated, a woman has been buried on the property on a long-forgotten gravesite. Somewhere within the confines of the amusement park's property is presumably a grave. As far as I can conclude, there was no paper trail for the woman's name, birth or death year. Unless I can find a name, I am afraid it would be near impossible to find the identity of the woman that is buried there.

My final angle was to cover the excavation that was done in the late 1980s. I finally made some headway with confirming that the amusement park did have an archaeological dig. The dig site is known as 'Snidow - 46MC01'. I put a call into Marshall University's Sociology and Anthropology Department where I did confirm with Dr. Nicholas Freidin (Marshall's lead archaeologist) that the dig sight known as 'Snidow – 46MC01' did, in fact, contain human remains, pottery, fire pits, foundations to buildings and an unprecedented wealth of artefacts from the 14th century. He also indicated that there was an additional find of pre-history artefacts which have been documented.

I also spoke to Lora Lamarre – Senior Archaeologist with West Virginia State Preservation Office – regarding the Snidow Dig. Lora also confirmed that the dig was reported and recorded as 'it contained a wealth of artefacts which included an entire village'. This dig was literally unprecedented in the number of intact artefacts and information that could be obtained from it regarding the Shawnee Indian Tribe.

It is very unfortunate that, due to personal reasons, Mr. White refuses any further examination of the property from a historical and archaeological approach. Instead of preserving this rich jewel to history, it has been flooded and turned into a catfish pond.

My final conclusion is this: the land in which the Lake Shawnee Amusement Park is situated has such a long and rich history, that the property should be legislatively mandated to be protected and available for current and future research by historians, anthropology and archaeological teams. The urban legend of the child dying from a traumatic swing incident is false. This is a hoax ghost story that was created within the past few years. Unfortunately, the West Virginia law does not encompass 'what is right'. It only details what a property owner's rights are. Currently, the legislation allows archaeologically and historically important properties to be used as the current owner sees fit. So, regardless of what treasures may lay on a man's land ... it's up to the landowner whether or not to allow said treasure to be preserved. The possibility of any haunting and/or paranormal activity is best explained with the next report from Rodney.

Personal experiences:
Mike Brown, Clayton Trout & Dr. Shari Stacy, Lake Shawnee Amusement Park, June 18, 2010. Investigators:

Mike, Clayton, Shari – personal experiences
Mike, Shari, and Clayton in field where tent is set up – about seventy-five yards from tent on the road in the direction of the house trailers:
No outstanding audio or images.
Personal experiences: At one point Mike asks, "Will you make a noise?" Both Shari and Mike heard a noise, which is noted at about 8:01 on audio 1-A-001 and noted on EVP log sheet given to Rodney Shortridge. Clayton did not hear the noise and the noise is not audible on the audio.

At about 9:30 on the audio all three investigators – Mike, Clayton, and Shari – all state that they hear a growl. Clayton and Mike question if it is traffic noise but, because of the location the growl seems to come from, they determine it is not coming from highway, but the field area of the property. The 'growl' is not audible on the recording.

Investigators hear murmuring coming from the direction of the tree line toward the trailers. The murmuring is not audible on recordings.

At tractor, 11:10pm:
Beginning at 1:46 into audio we began to get strong hits on the K2 meters. One K2 meter was positioned at the front of the tractor and the other K2 was positioned on the tractor seat. Both K2s received strong hits at different times in response to questions, which are audible on the recording. No EVPs were recorded on Shari's Sony recorder.

At 5:25 Shari asked if 'you want to play?, which initiates the strongest hit from the K2 meter positioned at the front of the tractor.

At swings:
One good hit on Mike's K2

Camera battery drain on both Clayton's and Mike's camera; both cameras had a full battery. Clayton's camera shut completely off several times. Battery level fluctuated on both cameras showing empty bars and then bars would show camera half charged.

Witnessed swing moving on its own.

Heather Lamantia
I was teamed with Matt O'Quin for this investigation. We were walking towards the pavilion area, just asking questions at random. From across the lake, over by swings and Ferris wheel, we heard what sounded like a female vice. At first we thought it may have been Amy Flick, who was also at amusement park area. It turned out she was only just a short distance away from us at the lake when it

happened. No other team members were there at the time. Not able to explain.

The most memorable experience was around the ticket booth area of the amusement park. In front of the booth, I began to smell buttered popcorn. It would come and go and in different spots; also got the smell at the big tree just across from the booth. Right in front of booth was the strongest smell for me.

I tried the swing test as the owner suggested. I held my hand about an inch over the swing that was indicated during the tour. The swing moved slightly. The chains seemed to twist at that time. Matt confirmed this; he also saw it happen. No other swings moved and no breeze was blowing. No contact with the swing itself with my hand or body. Not explained.

No experiences at Indian Village site.

Heather Lamantia 6-19-10

Evidence

Photo evidence: There are photos with unexplained orbs, unexplained lights and unexplained mist.

Video evidence: Of a K2 hit by one of the teams located at the swing set.

Note: BDPS does not support the idea of orbs as evidence of the paranormal because most orbs can be explained away as dust, bugs, rain, mist, fog, etc. There are cases in which the orbs we photograph seem to move with some type of intelligent intent. We post these photos because we feel that there needs to be more investigation into the 'Orb Phenomenon' and we shouldn't be so quick to dismiss this phenomenon without further investigation and explanation. So we show these photos in an attempt to add another piece to the puzzle and leave this decision up to you to accept or dismiss orbs as evidence. It is also my opinion that we should show all evidence so we all can learn from what might be an area of the paranormal that may be getting overlooked by researchers.

EVP's (Electronic Voice Phenomenon)
We heard the following EVP's (Electronic Voice Phenomenon) and unexplained noises on our DVR's (Digital Voice Recorders) & microcassette recorder:

Ferris wheel:
Unexplained click
Unexplained voice "Jeffery"
Unexplained male voice "What"

Ticket booth:
Unexplained 2 knocks
Unexplained girl's laugh
Unexplained footsteps
Unexplained loud click
Unexplained knock & footsteps

Tractor:
Unexplained male voice "Come up"

Mobile home (hot dog stand):
Unexplained breath
Unexplained voice "Hey"

Conclusion

We have come to the conclusion that the Lake Shawnee Amusement Park has very low paranormal activity, in the forms of EVPs, interesting photographic orbs, unexplained lights, mist, audio evidence and personal experiences that helped us to determine our conclusion.

With our conclusion, we would especially like to note that Lake Shawnee is located in a geographically unique area. The grounds are surrounded by mountains in this particular location, thus forming a bowl shape. In this type of setting, it is typical for the bowl-shaped geography to act as an "amphitheatre". This amphitheatre effect can distort the acoustics within the bowl itself. This can and does cause voices, traffic and typical everyday noises to be amplified. This, in turn, could explain some claims of disembodied voices.

Also, surrounding the park are two major highways,

Routes 10 and 19. As we witnessed on our investigation, these Routes are heavily travelled at night, explaining some of the 'unexplained lights' from previous claims. There is also a tree line and a creek that surrounds another large portion of the site, which separates the property and an adjacent mobile home park. With the combination of the amplified acoustics, the close proximity of the trailer-park and the constant highway noise, we conclude that most of the 'unexplained phenomena' surrounding this area can now more logically be explained.

As you can imagine, any traffic, voices, sounds and lights could potentially be bouncing back from the surrounding mountains and the tree line that surrounds the park. We look forward to one day coming back to investigate the Lake Shawnee Amusement Park with more advanced equipment. This was our twenty-second investigation and it was a great success. I feel honoured to have had the success we've had and to be working alongside such a professional team.

Personal thoughts by Rodney Shortridge, Founder of Black Diamond Paranormal Society (BDPS) on Lake Shawnee Amusement Park.

It is my opinion there needs to be a change immediately in the laws and legislation passed in the state of West Virginia to allow researchers, archaeologists and other individuals or groups with the knowledge and know-how to be allowed entry to any property to conduct archaeological digs and excavations of any Native American artefacts. I was extremely upset when I found out the Lake Shawnee Amusement Park property has significant historical artefacts of Native Americans and is a Native American burial ground, and there are no laws in place protecting these things in the state of West Virginia. I would like to see any property that has any type of significant amounts of Native American artefacts or burial grounds to be researched fully and to be protected by Tribal Nations. I would also like that any excavations that are done to fully restore the property as it was found and place the artefacts in museums or however the Tribal Nations see fit. I understand that as a property owner you want to protect your land and use it as you would like, but with extraordinary circumstances in cases such as this with a great amount of Native American history, an exception needs to be made. This would be a perfect opportunity for a property owner to have potential income from a museum depicting the artefacts found on their property. I've seen many museums in other parts of the United States that have great income potential for state and local municipalities. It saddens me greatly that Native American artefacts that have been covered in water for a fishing pond. I have Native American ancestry, as many Americans do, and I have a strong belief in preserving this part of our past and taking measures to do so. Our research has shown that the Lake Shawnee Amusement Park area has the potential to be one of the greatest archaeological finds on the East Coast as the previous limited research has shown. I would like this information to be shared with the remaining living tribal members who share in the ancestry and the state of West Virginia and the world. I feel that this property has an amazing story to tell other than the urban legends and other false tales that have been told about the area. While we conducted our paranormal investigation and knowing some history of the area there was a sense of a lost history there and its story needs to be told. While we conducted our paranormal investigation many of us felt we needed permission from the living members of the tribes and we were only granted permission to be there by the property owner. By profiting from ghost-seeking individuals, I believe this historical site has been desecrated. I feel this is a holy site that needs to be respected and honoured as such. I will be sending a copy of this report and also information about this site to the Tribal Nations in Washington, D.C. for their input, and to West Virginia congressmen, and all media outlets. This story needs to be heard by those who can make a difference

Final Report and Analysis
Case 023

Major Graham Mansion June 26, 2010
Max Meadows, Virginia

Investigators
Rodney Shortridge, Aaron Shortridge, Mike Brown, Matt
O'Quin, Heather Lamantia, Nathan Rasnick, along with
new members & honorary members
Micki Nelson, Clayton Trout & Dr. Shari Stacy, special
guests
Nick Ferra of Virginia Paranormal Society (VPS) and Kelly
Warf

On June 26th, 2010 the BDPS team investigated Major
Graham Mansion located in Max Meadows, Virginia. I
would like to take this moment to thank J.C. Weaver,
owner of the Major Graham Mansion; Mary Lin Brewer,
Director of the Major Graham Mansion; and Nick Ferra of
Virginia Paranormal Society, for giving us permission to
investigate such a historical site. We decided, because of
the size of the mansion and with the outbuildings that
consists of the slave house, general store, barn and the
yard surrounding the property, that each team would
investigate separate areas of the property and structures
simultaneously while one team would watch the camera
monitors at our base within the mansion.

We started our investigation around 6:00 pm with a
walking tour of the mansion that was given by Nick Ferra.
We started our set up around 7:00 pm We then proceeded
to our investigation soon after, dividing into teams. Team
one consisted of me and Matt O'Quin; Team two
consisted of Nathan Rasnick and Micki Nelson; Team
three consisted of Dr. Stacy and Clayton Trout; Team four
consisted of Aaron Shortridge and Kelly Warf; and Team
five consisted of Mike Brown and Heather Lamantia. Nick

Ferra assisted different teams throughout the night during the investigation. Each team was placed to investigate each of the buildings, with one team investigating the outside grounds surrounding the buildings, and one team monitoring our cameras back at base. Each team worked on a rotation, changing their location about every two hours. We finished our investigation around 6:00 am the following morning. This was a great experience and very helpful in our constant training.

EQUIPMENT USED AT THIS INVESTIGATION:
- (9) DVR's (Digital Voice Recorders)
- (3) microcassette recorders
- (4) Zero Lux low lever IR (infra-red) cameras
- Panasonic handheld camcorder
- Sony handheld camcorder
- Kodak digital cameras
- Nikon camera
- Fuji digital camera
- Canon digital camera
- Samsung digital cameras
- Motion diction IR (infra-red) field video/camera
- K2 meters
- EMF (Electro Magnetic Field) meter
- Laser thermometers

We placed one DVR (Digital Voice Recorder) in each of the areas of the property with reports or claims of paranormal activity; including the barn, general store, and slave house. In the mansion we placed one in the children's room, attic, master bedroom, pink room, basement, and the Bride's Room. The one IR camera was placed in the attic, one was placed in the children's room, one was placed in the master bedroom and one was placed in the Bride's Room. One Panasonic handheld camcorder was placed in the basement and one Sony handheld camcorder was placed in the kitchen. Three microcassette recorders were carried by three different teams during the investigation. Also, each team carried along with them during their investigations one of the following: K2 meter, EMF (Electro Magnetic Field) meter or laser thermometer.

Reports & claims:

There have been many tragic claims at this location that have allegedly ended in death, including the murder of Joseph Joel Baker in his cabin where the mansion is located today. According to court proceedings, Mr. Baker was killed by his slaves. On May 6th, 1784 the two slaves who were tried for Mr. Baker's murder were hung from a hickory tree on a hill overlooking the mansion. Local legend has it that these slaves roam the hills surrounding Cedar Run to this day. They were buried in unmarked graves on the property. A clairvoyant has made claims of a woman that is described as the "women in white" that looks out the window of a room on the second floor. This same clairvoyant is reported to have said that the woman is wearing a wedding dress, but these claims cannot be verified. Some speculate she is waiting for her fiancé who may have died during the Civil War. Many people have claims of hearing disembodied voices, being touched when no one touched them, seeing apparitions, objects moving on their own, the smell of pipe smoke when no one is smoking, and so on. The list is long, and this may be due to the large number of visitors throughout the world who come to this historical site to have a chance of experiencing such an amazing place.

In 2007, the Virginia Paranormal Society (VPS) began performing formal investigations at the mansion.

Over the course of three years, several paranormal groups have assisted VPS and collected hundreds of EVPs (i.e. electronic voice phenomena), and experienced paranormal contact at the mansion. VPS reports that many of its members have communicated with the dominant spirits of Martha Peirce Graham, Squire David Graham, and "Clara" a Civil War orphan who secretly lived (and died) at the mansion. In addition, we have a collection of ghost stories and photos from the community as well as anecdotal reports from guest clairvoyants. Is the mansion haunted? Come and decide for yourself!

Personal experiences:
Mike Brown, Nathan Rasnick & Micki Nelson

While doing the tour and walk-thru we were at Clair's room, I (Micki) and Mike were standing at the doorway and we both looked at each other and asked each other if we heard what the other one had. We both heard footsteps on the steps at her room. Mike went up and down the stairs and came back and told me no one was there.

Micki and Nathan had some activity in the Bride's Room. We heard knocking that sounded like someone was in the next room (Christmas Room), and it repeated itself on a couple of occasions. That was when Nathan called Rodney over the radio and he said we were the only ones in the house. After a while it quit and we were leaving the room. As Nathan walked out of the Bride's Room door, his right arm only had chill bumps and his hair was standing straight up on his arm. He said he felt as if someone walked right past him to go into the room. He took some pics of the room from the hallway and also some out in the hallway. 6/27/10

Heather Lamantia

I had two experiences that stand out on this investigation. The first experience occurred in the general store during the first round of the investigation. I was standing in front of the counter, around the middle, and Mike Brown was sitting on a wooden bench about two feet away. As I was standing there we were doing some EVP work. I felt a touch on my left ankle, on the inner part. I said something to Mike and he used a flashlight and K2 meter and detected nothing. We had resumed EVP work when I felt it again. Once again, Mike saw no trace of anything and no unusual K2 readings. He left the K2 at my feet after this and I felt it again. No traces.

Unfortunately, no K2 registered, partly because it had shut itself off at some point after he put it there. Never saw any insects or anything. This was always at same spot on my inner left ankle.

The second round of investigation, I had a second experience. I was in the Confederate Room while doing EVP work with Dr. Stacy. We were both sitting on the floor on the right side of the room (as you're entering the room on the right side). We were asking questions when I suddenly felt a chilly breeze on the left side of my body. I asked Dr. Stacy if she felt a breeze. She did not. We resumed questions. Once again I felt this same breeze along my left side. I asked some direct questions about this chilly breeze. I seemed to get a response with another chilly breeze at my side. We resumed our questioning, and I felt the breeze one last time. Dr. Stacy said she never felt a breeze in the room. The room was very stuffy; no windows open and no real way for a breeze to occur. I was not able to find a source for any breeze by natural causes.

These events are reported as truthfully as I recall them. 6/27/10

Rodney Shortridge & Matt O'Quin

First experience occurred while Matt and I were investigating the children's room. Matt was to my left, about six to eight feet away, sitting down, as was I. Clayton had placed a plasma ball in the middle of the room as an experiment to see if it would attract any response to the light and the energy that it creates. Matt and I were focused on the plasma ball and discussing Clayton's experiment. I began to notice a strange faint white light in almost a square shape. It was moving very fast and floating above the plasma ball. The light moved to the floor, up the wall, around the ceiling, and half way around the room before it disappeared; moving very fast at times and slow to the point of floating. I asked Matt, "Do you see that?"

His response was, "Yes, what the hell is that?" As I started to move from my chair, the light disappeared as fast as it had appeared. Matt and I checked the entire room with the K2 meter to see if we could find any electromagnetic field disruptions and there was none. No cold spots. Matt checked the hallway outside the door to the children's room to make sure no one was in the area with their flashlight on. There was no one in the hallway with a flashlight who could have done what we had seen. Even light from outside was investigated and there were no passing car lights and all members were in their investigating locations. The only other members in the house were Aaron and Kelly watching the camera monitors. I got on the radio and asked them did they see anything on the camera that was located in the room and they reported back they didn't see anything. We could not find any explanation for the light that we saw.

Second experience occurred while Matt, Nick and I were in the general store investigating. While in the general store, Nick was sitting behind the counter about six feet away in front of me, Matt was to my left about eight feet away, sitting on a bench – as was I. We were doing EVP work and asking questions and waiting for a response to one of the questions I had asked, "Do you know the town or county that was once called Jeffersonville?" That is where I live. It is now called Tazewell and the county is also called Tazewell. Within a few seconds of my question we got a surprise response of a growl and everyone in the room heard it. I replied, "So, I take it you don't like the town?" Again, we heard a low growl. Matt and Nick investigated the area while I went outside to check around the store to make sure there weren't any animals nearby that may have made the growling sound. As I investigated the outside of the building, I could not find any animals, or explanation for the sound we heard. I went back inside to check with Matt and Nick to see if they found any evidence that could explain what we heard, and they explained to me that they also could not find the source of the growl. This was an interesting experience for which we have no explanation. 6/27/10

Evidence

Photo evidence: There are photos with unexplained orbs and a dark area covering a child's ball in the children's room.

Video evidence: an unexplained figure or apparition walking outside by the basement door. Later, an orb can be seen that appears and disappears near the same door in the basement.

Note: BDPS does not support the idea of orbs as evidence of the paranormal because most orbs can be explained away as dust, bugs, rain, mist, fog, etc. There are cases that the orbs we photograph seem to move with some type of intelligent intent. We post these photos because we feel that there needs to be more investigation into the Orb Phenomenon and we shouldn't be so quick to dismiss this phenomenon without further investigation and explanation. So we show these photos in an attempt to add another piece to the puzzle and leave this decision up to you to accept or dismiss orbs as evidence. It is also my opinion to show all evidence so we all can learn from what might be an area of the paranormal that may be getting over looked by researchers.

EVPs (Electronic Voice Phenomenon)

We heard the following EVPs (Electronic Voice Phenomenon) and unexplained noises on our DVRs (Digital Voice Recorders) & microcassette recorder:

Attic:
Unexplained knocks (2)
Unexplained breaths (2)
Unexplained sound, maybe bullfrog
Unexplained noise
Unexplained breath and knock
Basement:

Unexplained noise
Unexplained female whisper (indecipherable)
Unexplained knocking and a yell
Unexplained whisper ("Hey") and a click
Unexplained whisper (indecipherable)
Bride's Room:
Unexplained whisper (indecipherable)
Children's Room:
Unexplained female voice (Justin)
Unexplained noise
Unexplained knock
Unexplained loud bang
Unexplained whisper (Brad)
Unexplained whisper and a low moan or whisper
Unexplained loud click
Unexplained noise (sounds like something drops and hits the floor, but no one was in the house at the time).
Master Bedroom:
Unexplained voice
Unexplained scratching, breath and whisper
Unexplained voice (indecipherable)
Unexplained female voice ("Right")
Slave House:
Unexplained noise
Unexplained footsteps

Conclusion

We have come to the conclusion that the Major Graham Mansion has very high paranormal activity in the forms of EVPs, interesting photographic orbs, unexplained dark mass, audio and video evidence which showed an unexplained apparition, and unexplained formation of lights or orbs and personal experiences that helped us to determine our conclusion.

ARROW HEAD PARANORMAL is a group I found both on Facebook and Twitter. These stories have been given by Chad Saunders who is a member of the team. They are based in Norwich, Connecticut and have shared these following stories.

This is my first story I would like to tell you about; it took place at what has become known as "The Demon House" – it has featured in various TV shows and is in Enfield, Connecticut.

It is a really creepy duplex house; when one previous owner bought the place he thought it would be a good idea to remove one of the walls, which has resulted in a very strange layout as it now has two sets of stairs right next to each other.

So, our team went along, and we took a mother and daughter pairing of empaths with us, which really helped a lot as they could verify what we were hearing were spirits and not just some creaking of floorboards. Snow, the young daughter, and her mother belong to a team called 'Crossing the Veil Paranormal' and are very good at what they do.

Some of the investigators were up on the second floor and the pair of empaths were trying to get a spirit to cross over (we have good photographic evidence of this); at the same time this was going on, one of the guys investigating with us started to feel hands round his throat and choking him. He actually had finger marks on his throat and he was starting to freak out. He was kicking out at something none of us could see, even himself, but the results were there in front of us. The rest of the team, who were downstairs, rushed up to him as soon as we heard what was going on, at the same time turning on the lights as we went.

The night we went to this house, it was about November time I think, and it was very cold outside, the house had no heating on but, in the room the guy was getting choked in, the temperature registered at 100 degrees! He managed to free the hands that had been around his throat, at the same time he was doing this we were filming it all, or so we thought, but the batteries in the camera had drained completely, although they were on full charge just a very short while before. The battery drain was a frequent happening that night, on more than just the cameras. The investigator had by that time gone outside for air and to get himself back together and, after a while – we were out there with him – we decided that we should just go back in and do what we had set out to do.

We went back in, but I had to connect my camera to the mains as the battery drain was continuous, but my lead wasn't long enough to reach upstairs, so we went back to the hand-held cameras. Brittany, one of our investigators, soon started to flip out by kicking stuff around; this was not like her at all and we thought it best if we took her outside for a break too. While we were outside we took the precaution of "sageing" her and we gave her a few minutes to recover as she was crying. My friend Dave's daughter was with us, and she got upset and started crying. Snow (the younger empath) said that whatever it was seemed to be going after the weaker people in the group. Personally, I had no problems and she said that was because I didn't believe in it; that was why it didn't want me. It went only after people who truly believed.

We were there for about four hours in all and in that time we went through about sixty batteries, in everything from voice recorders to cameras. This was our first big case and, yes, we will be going back!

This next investigation I was not on, personally. It took place at the Wishing Well house, which is an old plantation property situated in New Milford.

It was a horrible night in November when the team went to the house and it was freezing cold. It was one of those nights when any bit of equipment they had with them malfunctioned; if it could go wrong, it did.

As the owner of the house, Greg, came in to speak to us, something tripped him. He hit the ground so hard he got a split head and within seconds he had an egg-sized lump come up. Looking for what he had tripped over, the team found nothing was to be seen. One of the guys in the team is an Emergency Medical Technician (EMT) and he took him to hospital to make sure he hadn't got a concussion.

As I said, it was a horrible night; the Team were getting all kinds of crazy readings on their various bits of apparatus. Walls that should have a temperature of near freezing were showing on the thermal camera at 144 degrees. The image was showing fire red. Pictures of this are available if anyone wants to have a look. On the wall there wasn't even a heating vent to make it read as it did.

Another room situated upstairs is one called the Master's Quarters; the slave quarters and slave kitchen being downstairs. In the rooms in this area the team got some of the best photographic evidence we have ever captured on any investigation. There are orbs moving like I have never seen before. I am not usually a believer in orbs, as I think that they can be explained as mainly dust or bugs. But, the way this thing moved was totally different to any that I have seen before or since! It came toward you then stopped and spun around then went off in another direction entirely. I can't explain it. We ran the film through Adobe and other programmes (I worked for Apple for over thirty years), and we cannot figure out what it was. The night was completely amazing, apart from Greg getting hurt.

There are various spirits in the house, one is a little girl called Sarah. There is an older spirit man who likes young girls; he likes to grab at them. I absolutely love the house and love doing public investigations there. There is so much activity in the place. We have conducted maybe five or six public investigations in the house, which include one with John Zaffis and other prominent investigators.

My third story is about the New London House. This was the place that really freaked me out and I don't do that very easily!

The house is occupied and the family have two kids. The kids started to draw some very strange and worrying pictures, showing a guy with very long hair. It turns out that this house used to be a boarding house and that a guy who lived there had actually died in the room that was now used as the mother's bedroom. It came to light that he had been a child molester in life and, even now, he likes to talk to the kids and make grabs at the women in the house. The kids weren't just drawing pictures; they started talking about things that they should have been too young to know anything about, asking questions too. That was when we got asked to go in.

The house is huge and has a barn out the back, so we went into the house and placed cameras where we could. We went into the property with the empaths; soon after they started to freak out as they said that there was something following them around. At one point we went outside and someone got a really hard push; so hard that they fell over. Of course, there was nothing there to have made them trip when we checked.

The younger one of our empaths kept telling us to, "Go by the water;" there is a pond out by the barn. The Spirit Box also told us to "go into the water". At this point I looked back at the house and in one of the second storey windows I saw the silhouette of a man; this is where all the activity had been taking place. As I watched, he turned to the side and walked in front of a second window. Crap, I thought, as typically I didn't have my camera running at the time, I was really unhappy about that.

We decided we should go back inside and go and check out the very unique basement area. I say that as it has a cell, which is the best way to describe it, in the middle of the floor. It has no door on it and inside it has spaces for what could be beds. Snow and Taylor, our empaths, were trying to seal the place and wanted our team to help them. We caught many EVPs down there and I think this is one of my best places to have investigated.

Another story that comes to mind that I would like to share is the Elington House. It has so much activity we have to keep going back. It is quite a poor area and has a very strange atmosphere. This property also has a peculiar atmosphere, in the basement especially.

So, we went there. This time we took a medium with us. Now, I have a rule that we don't tell them anything about the place where we are going to, not even the place it is in, so they can't do any research on the place before we get there. The way I see it is: if they are any good at what they do, then they can pick it up at the location when we get there!

The psychic walked in and immediately said, "Whoa! Stop! I am picking up on the most terrible energy here." He didn't want to go into the basement, but we had to make him go to make out what he could sense down there. We told him that, by acting like he was, he was scaring the client (who was with us) even more than they were already.

The client had heard lots of screams coming from the basement, which to us was kind of freaky anyway! Before we had come to this house, our historian had done some checking and had turned up some information which said that in the 1890s, the owners had two disabled children who they put in the basement as they were ashamed of them; they lived down there all alone and all of the time. They were never allowed upstairs.

Today, in the basement, you can see a room down there which is where these poor kids were kept. Their parents thought that they should never have been born and couldn't care less about them. The historian found that they had died from lack of water. Well, it seemed that those poor kids didn't even know they were dead; they did, however, know we were there, but didn't know when they were. The psychic was talking to them and explaining what had happened to them and was trying to get them to cross over.

This was a very sad case. I think we did actually help those kids. I touched base with the owners a couple of years ago, they told me it was pretty quiet down there now. I was so happy to hear that and was happy that we helped in the way we did.

Again, a story that comes to mind is about a house which again was occupied at the time in a place called Mountville.

We had been asked to go there as the lady said that her two kids were having trouble sleeping as there was a woman who kept poking them while they were in bed.

So, we got there, and the kids showed us some pictures that they had drawn of the woman; they said she has a mean feeling about her, she had long white hair and NO EYES! There were just black spaces where they should have been. We all thought the same thing – this is getting interesting!

We took base readings all through the house as we went; we also did EMFs and the temperature of the walls. As we went into the basement we got loads of hits down there. The Spirit Box was going off almost all the time with a voice telling us to "get out!" I am not a fan of the Spirit Box, I am very sceptical about it; by far the EVPs are my favourite. The Spirit Box kept insisting we get out and we decided that may be a good idea, so we headed off to the kids' room to investigate there.

There were three of our investigators who became totally overwhelmed by what they were feeling in that room, so we thought it best to leave there. I decided that I would go back in on my own. Inside it was pitch black, but in I went and closed the door. My second-in-command came in at that point and straight away said, "Whoa, whoa, whoa!" I said, "What's up?" He said, "There is a lady standing in front of you and staring at you!" So, I asked him, "What does she want?" He said, "You're not scared of her?" I had no reason to be – I couldn't see her! He said, "She's staring you down!" Then he said, "She is backing off now and going under the bed."

After the investigation there, my historian sent me an email about the property. Our psychic also told us the woman didn't speak much, but she did find out that the woman had lived there. She didn't want kids in that room; she didn't mind kids, just not in there. It seems the woman had passed away in that bedroom in the forty somethings and that the room had also been used as a sewing room as she had been a seamstress and some kids had trashed the place one day. She was stuck protecting what she still regarded as her room, so we helped her to cross over too.

Almost a year ago, I contacted the family who had asked us there. It seems the kids are fine now and everything has settled down. The kids don't have nightmares anymore and it is all quiet now. It seems we did a good job for her and the woman we crossed over.

My last story is about a house in Groton which is owned by a very religious Spanish family.

I hadn't been with this team for long, but I must say that this was one of the weirdest places I have been in a long time!

I was sitting alone in one of the rooms and checking the equipment, making sure the camcorder worked and all the equipment we were going to use had full batteries in them. Now, this sounds like a total cliché: I am sitting concentrating on doing my work when – suddenly – loads of TOYS start coming round the corner! I turned the camcorder towards them and suddenly the batteries (which were brand new and checked as fully charged) went dead. Totally drained!

Every hair I have on my body stood on end. I quickly walked out of the room, and went to find another investigator who was in another room and sitting on a bed.

As I told her about what had happened, we caught an EVP which said "take them away", as clear as day. We both went upstairs and started to talk to whatever it was.

As I said, the family who lived there were very religious, and started to get very worried about what was happening, so she (the investigator), went to the kitchen with them, taking her Sprit Box. I didn't go with her at that time, but stayed upstairs.

Suddenly I could hear her screaming from the kitchen at what the Box was saying, which was: "Chad ... Raymos ... Chad kill Raymos ... Kill ... Black bag, blue knife ... Black bag, blue knife". I thought "Holy shit! How can this be saying all the same things over and over?" A Spirit Box only works on scrolling radio waves; it shouldn't be able to do this! That freaked me the hell out! I mean, it scared me!

At this point, we went back into the bedroom and I set the camera up and we started an EVP session. We got all kinds of hits. I noticed at this point that everyone was standing on one side of the room, by the door. I was sitting down close to the wall, near the window. Then a guy came in and was smiling at me – weird.

After a while, we left the room and the guy who had been smiling at me came over and said, "I just want to say that it was really cool that you sat by that wall."

So, I said, "What are you talking about?"

He said, "Weren't you listening?"

"No – why?" I said.

Turns out one of the kids who lived there said that he had seen what he described as a "veil" and that something was trying to take him through it. Like from the movie, *Insidious*, just like that is what he described. It freaked me out a bit, but then I thought that maybe they were just trying to play about with us?

After what I and the team saw and heard in that house, the family contacted a priest and he went over to bless it, but that made their situation even worse, to the point where the family couldn't stand it any longer and they moved out. Whatever it was had been focusing on their autistic son. The husband called us to go back to help, but the wife didn't want us to as she was scared we would piss it off even more.

The house had an effect on everyone; the family were crying and some team members too. We did get some of our best ever EVPs there, but everyone was very emotional. I didn't feel that way; it seems not to affect me. I just freaked out. Something wanted us the hell out of there. I just couldn't stay there; it is unusual for me to have that type of reaction, but I had to leave.

This had to be one of the best places I have ever investigated. Something wanted us and the family out – it got its wish.

This next offering is from Aaron Colliver of the North Cornwall Paranormal team, based in the UK, who also contributed to my previous books. This is a personal experience from Aaron.

Before I was a member of North Cornwall Paranormal team, I investigated many locations on my own. One of these is a small church yard in Mid Cornwall. At this location there is a rare type of granite, which is only found at this precise location. It contains a higher amount of quartz in the stone and, if you are familiar with crystals, then you will know that they are supposed to hold energy in them. This was the reason I was drawn to this location, assuming: more crystal – more energy.

It was a late November night, the temperature was minus fifteen degrees and a fine layer of frost covered the grass within the church yard. When I arrived, I could feel the presence of several spirits following me. I did a preliminary sweep with my K2 meter, with the result of no anomalies. I decided then to get out my EVP recorder and start rolling. All this was when I was new to investigating and would record the whole of the investigation on the digital recorder, just to make sure I didn't miss any possible communication through an EVP.

I decided to sit with my back to the stone wall of the church and speak out into the church yard. Within minutes of sitting down, I started to hear noises all around me. The night was very still; the air was crisp. In the darkness I started to hear footsteps crunching on the frozen grass. As I was hearing this, I carried on calling out saying, "Come as close as you would like. I am not scared of you, so you shouldn't be afraid of me either. You are more than welcome to use as much of my energy as you like, if it helps you to communicate with me."

Then, within a matter of minutes, the footsteps stopped. I felt I was being surrounded by a group of people but only that I couldn't see them. At this point I started to hear funny squeaks, which I put down to contamination as it almost sounded like a fox in the far distance. This carried on for an hour or so, then it all seemed to stop. No more sounds, no more footsteps – nothing. The feeling of being surrounded lifted too. At this point I decided to relocate to another part of the church yard.

After another hour of asking questions, it seemed that whatever was with me at the previous location had left and now I was on my own. It was now getting late and I was nearly losing sensation in my toes, so I decided it was time to go home.

As soon as I stepped into my house, I got out the EVP recorder to start listening back to what I might have captured, with anticipation. From the second I turned it on I had captured many spirits, which all seemed to be speaking at the same time! The first voice I had captured was a gentleman with a deep, husky voice. He responded to my question of, "Is there any message that you would like me to give someone?" with "Harrietta, I'm sorry". The word "sorry" was dragged out. This was amazing! My first spirit voice was an intelligent one; I was so excited! I couldn't sleep and had to listen to see if I had caught more. I wasn't disappointed!

At the point that I was sitting by the church, I had captured many voices, just talking to me. After I had just asked out for a name, I got a chap as clear as anyone standing next to me saying "John Pink". My mind was blown, to say the least! For the whole time I was there I was capturing spirits talking to me and also amongst themselves. As I had been walking around, it seems that a gentleman was asking other spirits for help, saying "Please follow them" to try and get my attention. I could write a fair few paragraphs about all the voices I caught on that night.

I would like to finish by saying that, out of all the locations I have ever investigated, this one has its own individual energy that I have yet to experience anywhere else. Is it due to the quantities of crystal in the stone? I am unsure and cannot say for certain, but it did seem that way. I am constantly drawn back to this place to try and gain more answers to its buried secrets.

This next story is from some kind guys who contributed to both of my previous books. They started to put together their own book with all of their previous investigations included. They are a team made up of friends and family. They are a really tight team and they have given me permission to use anything I would like from their book. I have chosen this one as it is their first real investigation and is a little different in the fact it is told by multiple members, and what each of them experienced personally. Keegan Cool is the lead narrator of this case.

By February of 2008, word had slowly begun to creep out that we had started investigating at haunted locations and, on a very cold and snowy night, we performed our first public investigation – and our first outdoor investigation as well.

Mark: I was over at Keegan and Colin's house for the

night, as we had been planning to do an investigation at Memmen Ridge Open Space in Castle Rock, Colorado. This is a local beauty spot and used for hiking and general leisure activities.

Colin: Some of Mom's work friends tagged along for the night too. We had been surfing the Web and discovered Memmen Ridge on the website 'Shadowlands', where it said that people reported hearing voices of children, which were believed to be from when a guy took a group of kids up into the woods and they all burned to death. Enough to say we were intrigued.

Keegan: Mom had some work friends over, as Colin said, which included Coreen and her daughter. They had also become interested in seeing what other-worldly things were happening on the ridge.

Night fell and we packed ourselves and equipment into two cars; it was quite a large group that night, and we made our way ten minutes north to Memmen Ridge.

We parked, and I think the three of us (Colin, Mark and I) practically jumped out, raring to begin. It was chilly, but clear skies and eight-plus inches of snow. It was perfect conditions for the investigation. Now, I'll be honest: I really didn't have too much faith in the possibility of catching something.

Colin: Our first stop was at the bridge over the stream that was purported to be the location to try to hear the voices of children.

Keegan: We didn't hear much at all.

Mark: We actually debunked the voices as noise pollution, as apartments were maybe a few hundred feet away, and felt the voices could have come from them.

Keegan: Yes, we all believed it to be noise pollution, which was unfortunate but, up to this point, the investigation was going as expected; not too well, at least in the respect of finding anything.

We decided to venture further on into the woods; the dark canopy of the pine trees put an ominous feeling into most everyone. It felt dark; mysterious; maybe even a little brooding at this point.

We hiked deeper into the forest, something made a little harder by the amount of snow and the rather steep incline at the start. The forest opened up into a small clearing after the incline, but soon returned to a more forested type of environment.

We walked until the path was out of sight, and decided to do an EVP session. At this point I was in front; Mark, who had the video camera, was second; and Colin was third with the still camera.

We asked our normal questions like "What is your name" and "Why are you here?"; the basics for any session. Mark carefully documented every second. It seemed rather quiet up to this point, so we ventured even further into the forest. That's when things started to become odd: we heard noises here and there and we encountered the occasional cold spot, which is saying something because of how cold it already was!

We also started to hear voices and that's when we all started to become excited. The voices were not like if you were having a conversation; they were at least distinct, but they almost had a radio-like sound to them. It's hard to describe what they sounded like, but their tone was almost static; like, very electrical; almost a tinny quality to them. Not normal, to say the least.

Brush would begin to move, and we got a strange feeling of being drawn towards a tree (one we would later find out was referred to as the hanging tree) so we did some investigations around that and the surrounding hills; we soon realized that the forest had become rather quiet, and that it was seemingly done for the night.

It had been a very exciting location, but we didn't stop there.

Colin: One of Mom's friends suggested going to investigate at an abandoned house not even ten minutes away. Not much was known about this house, other than

145

the fact people experienced weird shadows while they were in it. What I remember about the house is a bat flying straight at me! I thought someone had thrown it at me.

Mark: Don't forget about the pigeons that also flew at us!

Keegan: Yes, well, besides both of the animal incidents, the night went pretty smoothly there.

Exploring for a little while, we saw the house had weird writings on the walls. Some of it was in English; some not. There was something brown splattered on some of the walls.

The weeds had grown inside the house; the windows had been knocked out and some walls seemed to have met with a sledge hammer. The house had a vibe to it, but we didn't stay too long there that night, though we would eventually go back.

We headed home, and that's when the amazing stuff happened.

Colin: We caught Lawrence.

Mark: What about the ghost standing next to you and Colin?

Keegan: The evidence played out well. I was excited, to say the least, to see what we had caught. It was amazing.

Firstly, our findings from Memmen Ridge. We caught our most famous EVP that night – "Lawrence".

On the EVP we heard Keegan say, "What is your name?" The response was "Lawrence". What made this even cooler was the fact that, on the video at the same time, something manifests near the top of the hill then it shoots down towards the group, slowly turning towards the EVP recorder, after Keegan said, "What is your name?" To catch something that clear – not only as an EVP, but also a spirit on video – made it almost surreal. It felt to all of us a once in a lifetime capture. It's also something that is documented on our YouTube channel, as we have a video showing the Lawrence evidence.

Mark: It looks like a face when you see it.

Colin: Yes, it does. On the TV you can see it very clearly.

Keegan: As Mark said earlier, you can see a spirit manifest during the video next to me and Colin. We are standing out in the open, then, all of a sudden, a girl is standing next to us, but hiding in the bushes. All we could see was an outline of her; no distinct features.

The last of the evidence looked like someone riding a bike back and forth through the forest; just a quick moving shadow, which, while cool, pales in comparison to the first two pieces of evidence we caught.

The evidence coming from the abandoned house was also perplexing. The recorder picked up an angry-sounding wind blowing; so loud it made hearing a train that passed by nearly impossible. The strange thing is, there wasn't any wind that night; it was clear and quiet all the while we investigated. But not on the EVP – the wind was loud until we got into the building (which had no windows) when it died down. That was the point where we got the EVP of a dog barking. Yes, we caught a dog barking!

This is also on our YouTube channel. The dog barking EVP is amazing, and shows, we believe, ghosts can also be animals, not just people.

I think this night was very important to us all – not only in being our first public investigation, our first outdoor investigation, or our first investigation at a place we had never been to before – but important in what evidence it gave to us.

To this day, Lawrence is our best evidence we have ever caught; it's a remarkable find. We would try to find him again (as we told in Erica's first two books: 'Ghosts, Demons & Dolls' and 'Angels, Ghosts and Demons') but we never have, since that first case there. The abandoned house we did make it back to, but the dog EVP would never be caught again; both of those two are some of my favourite bits of evidence captured by us to date, and the reason we keep striding forward, with the aim to find out more about the Paranormal field and everything it encompasses.

Jill (Colin and Keegan's mum), also recalls about this investigation that it was in the winter and there were a large group who went to investigate while there was still snow on the ground. This is her version of what she saw and what happened there.

Jill: The boys were at the front; Keegan, Mark and Colin with the recording and video equipment; and rest of the group and I were at the back. Someone in my group had a camera. I remember that the boys started to ask questions like "Is there anyone here with us?" and "What is your name?"; the basic questions. They heard nothing in response and didn't see anything either. So we all moved a little further on. Not too much happened, really. At least, until the video and sound was reviewed back at home!

No one saw anything at the time, but, on the video, you could see a manifestation of a person, you can see its face, and at the same exact time on the audio recording you hear a voice say very plainly "Lawrence".

At another spot at the same location, they also caught something that no one saw while we were all there. The video shows Keegan and Colin standing next to each other, and at the same time you can clearly see the complete figure of an apparition standing next to them. It is a man wearing a hat, similar to a hat an Amish man would wear. They didn't see it at all. However, they did hear some noises and had the feeling that somebody was watching them, but nothing was seen at the time. This was only apparent when we all reviewed the footage. When we checked the timing on the film, it was exactly the same time that we heard the name "Lawrence".

This was one of the very first investigations that the boys did, and they needed somewhere to store their equipment, so I went down to the thrift store and got some bags for them. I also bought a briefcase for the more expensive equipment, so it wouldn't get damaged. When I got them home, I looked inside the briefcase and there was a paper in it. I took it out and looked at it and it was a birth certificate.

The name on it was for a man called Lawrence!

This next story is from a lady called Dawn. I know her well as she was married to my cousin, who this story is about. I only found out about this a few weeks ago. I think you could certainly classify this as an EVP.

I had been with Jaeger since I was just sixteen years old. He was one of three children. He had another brother and a sister. When I got to my twenties, Jaeger and I moved to Wales, which is where I am originally from. We had a nice life and were in the process of doing up a sweet little cottage in the country; then we found out that his brother had an inoperable kidney problem and shortly after he died.

We were both very sad at this news and, to pile on more stress not too long after, Jaeger was diagnosed with having a rare blood disorder. It was very serious and after many years of treatments, which in the main were unsuccessful, he too passed away.

He knew his time was coming and he made video tapes for members of the family, which he made me promise to give to them once he had passed. A couple of months before he passed on, we decided that we would get married. It was something we both had wanted, but never seemed to have got around to doing. He was very matter-of-fact about that he wouldn't be with me much longer, and we made plans as to what we would like to happen when the time came. He was enormously brave about it.

We still tried to make the best of everything, including doing the house up and buying new carpets and rehanging doors. He wanted me to have a comfortable home for when he was no longer with me. I had an accident one day with some bleach, and spilled a bit on the new carpet. If he had been well, he would have gone mad! But he didn't; he just took it all in his stride and never even lost his temper a little bit. This was pretty unusual as he could be quite feisty about things, especially before he became so ill.

It wasn't long before the illness got the better of him and he passed away. I was devastated, even though we both knew it was going to happen. It was good he wasn't suffering any more, but I didn't know what I was going to do without him. Family and friends were a great support.

My sister and I are quite spiritual people and she had booked for both of us to go and see a psychic medium on the Monday after the funeral. It was too soon for me to think of anything like that and I told her I wasn't going with her. She understood and said she would call me if Jaeger came through. Well, he did contact her and she phoned me saying that he had been speaking about things in the house he had not got around to finishing, like the doors. He also mentioned the bleach on the carpet.

We were chatting about things and suddenly there was a very loud "HELLO". The voice was unmistakeable: it was Jaeger's voice; it was very distinctive and quite a gravelly voice, just as he used to sound! My sister asked who it was. I told her it was Jaeger, although he did sound like he was talking through static and it had a hollow sound too. But it was his voice; no doubting it.

My sister said she would hang up the phone and I said I would hang on after to see if I could hear him again. She hung up and I stood there for ages, asking if he was there; could he hear me? But there was nothing after that one word – just silence.

It had been a total shock to me, and I called my sister and told her that I had nothing else to tell her; that was it, just the word "Hello".

A few years later, I met my current husband and we have two lovely children, a boy and a girl. Ruby is my oldest and one night, as I was putting her to bed, we were just getting her settled and the dog came in to stay with her, when she looked at the space at the top of the stairs and, plain as day, she said, "Goodnight Jaeger." I am sure she could see him, although of course she never knew him. She was often playing with someone no one else could see, whoever it was made her laugh a lot. I am sure it was him.

This is a short story from Clive Cowan; he got in touch as I had put out a request for stories in Facebook. He is from Omagh, County Tyrone in Northern Ireland.

I had been out with three of my friends, Wesley Irwin, Pearce Fox and Kyle Barton, for a day of golfing at Ardglass Golf club. We decided when we had finished playing to go to the clubhouse to finish off the day.

After a short while, we decided that we would go up to the second floor where the snooker room was situated and have a few games before going home. All the time we were playing, we could hear people talking in the room next to us. It sounded as if they were holding a meeting of some sort. A few games of snooker later, we decided to go home. We left them to the meeting they were having, with no snooker ball noises to interrupt them.

We got downstairs and the bar person was just going around getting ready to lock up for the night; it was about eight in the evening by this time. We told him that there were still people up in the meeting room next to the snooker room. He looked at us rather strangely and told us that we were the last ones there, and that there was no one else in the rooms upstairs or the building. But we had clearly heard them talking all the time we were playing. There was only one entrance to the meeting room and it was through the room we were playing in. There was a TV downstairs but it wasn't switched on, so it couldn't have been that we heard, and I don't think we would have heard it from two floors away anyhow.

All the time we were hearing the talking, we were not particularly concerned. It was only when we got downstairs and was told we were the only ones there we realized it was pretty unusual. However, Ardglass golf club is a very old building and has some history of ghostly tales and happenings and it seems we had just been witness to another one! To this day we would all swear to what we had heard that evening.

I saw these guys on Facebook, hope you enjoy this offering I got from them. It shows how every group who investigate do things just a little bit differently.

GhostÉire, a paranormal psychic research group has been established for the past ten years; we define ourselves as spiritual sympathizers, consultants and explorers with radically prepared experiments. This limits the amount of investigations, but yields a more intense operation, trying to discover and learn more in great detail of the differences between our distance and theirs.

In the past few years, we believe we have gained knowledge through meditation, prophetic, instinct and other means, prior to visiting numerous historic landmarks by contacting our Spirit guides.

To us, these beings have different powers and methods, which dictate how we should go about a paranormal investigation; from what questions to ask, in a particular language, at a particular area, with which experiment to use, along with any other information that could prove a pinnacle to how our time (or the Spirit's time) at the location should be spent.

We call upon these Spirit guides for direction, protection and clear answers before, during and even after an investigation, and in our daily lives.

I, Anthony Kerrigan, know that these energies are ever-present. I personally have a way of assurance, with a code to signify I am ready for their intervention.

Other GhostÉire members, Sinead, John Paul and Cameron, have abilities in the sense of feeling, intuition, meditation and knowing what words to phase in.

I haven't seen a ghost, or have I? I tend to hear them. Jen, my wife, has seen them in full-colour modern day attire.

It was on an island investigation, a few years ago, walking back to the campsite on a boreen road, noted locally to have been associated with the resting place of so many souls who died in the Great Famine (1845-1852), that she described unease. She could see these figures, quite clearly, in coloured clothing.

It was an uneventful investigation with the sessions, the equipment and the various gadgets being used, failing to pick up anything significant, except for the fact several of the team were affected mentally; from being disorientated, drowsiness or being weirded out, which might relate to the condition of possession.

In one case, an investigation we did in a theatre in County Waterford, I did have a personal experience which could have gone either way.

The team and I were in the rehearsal room, up above the main theatre. The talking board was used to communicate. We had composed a few questions a couple of days beforehand.

I asked, "Do you have a message for us?"

The Planchette (divination device) moved to, 'I' 'N', 'Y' 'O' 'U', 'I', 'C' 'O' 'U' 'L' 'D', 'L' 'I' 'V' 'E'. I wasn't taken aback by the statement, but felt intrigued.

Later that evening, in the darkened, empty-seated theatre, we had set up a table on the stage for a séance. There was only three of the team in the theatre; another team member, Cameron, was on his own in the dressing room, a good distance away, looking into a mirror (scrying), signalling any presences to come forth.

Meanwhile, Sinead and I connected at the table; Jen was recording at the time.

Sinead was getting visions and names coming into her head; I did as well. We both called out, asking for the table to move more, trying to get a big reaction. My head was uncontrollably twitching, mostly to my left … something was about to make itself be known.

Sinead called out, "Describe who you are, say your name?"

Looking back on the night vision camera which Jen was holding, it could be seen that my right hand started to contort, my ring finger pointing upwards.

"Whisper your name?" Sinead asked.

I briefly lost control of my right hand; it came off the table. For a short few seconds I stop twitching. Then my head twitches to the left one last time and I begin to retch. My gagging reflexes are prominent, and I let out a deep groan.

On the recording, the words, "It's slave boy" are assumed to have come out from my very own lips.

All that I can remember is that I am very aware in my mind that I am present, but I have no control over my body. A slight dizziness, like that split second when you experience the world spinning around as you are about to throw up.

After the words were spoken, I let out a long groan, which continued into an agonising sigh.

My fingers and thumbs are now bent, pointing upward, but the palms of my hands are still flat on the surface of the table. I am gasping for air, with my mouth wide open. I take one large inhale; my right leg is stretched out behind me, to my right hand side.

All that I can remember is my young son, Stoker. This image in my head and the intervention of Jen shining an ultraviolet torch on my face made the condition subside. Sweating and face down on the table, I get hold of my bodily functions and leave the theatre to get some fresh air outside.

Peculiar footsteps also could be heard on the recordings in the dressing room at that precise time where Cameron was Scrying.

At no point did I feel in any danger. Maybe this goes back to having faith in Spirit guides. Possession, perhaps?

Well, going back to the point, was I fearful? You could say 'yes', but accepting it meant it was a form of channelling, otherwise sharing. I believe it is how we deal with the situation.

Some would blame the talking board, but if we are to explore we have to break the boundaries and hearsay. We have been using it for years now. I treat what occurred that night as a learning curve, and a way of reaching out for more.

The conditions that night were probably perfect for that experience to happen. In other ways, it hasn't happened since like that, and I don't know if it will happen again.

So, that is almost the end of this book but … I have one more story for you from another well-known name in the paranormal field. This is from Barri Ghai, who is a co-presenter on 'Help! My House is Haunted!' He has been on other TV shows and is also very into tech when it comes to investigating and I thank him very much for this contribution. He has his own team called The Ghostfinder Paranormal Society and describes himself as a professional investigator.

My parents divorced when I was just five. My dad moved out and met someone who I eventually considered a second mother to me and my younger sister Serena. At the age of around fifteen, my father and stepmother moved to a house in near Windsor. It was called Oak Tree house and was a modern, detached, four-bedroomed family home in Berkshire.

At weekends and school holidays I would stay with them and my two much younger half-sisters, Lucy and Georgia, and occasionally my sister would join me for a visit. I didn't have a bedroom of my own but slept in the guest room at the top of the house. The room was quite large and had a king-size bed nested at one end where the eves of the roof sloped down towards the bed.

The room was nicely decorated and well furnished with bookcases, built-in wardrobes and shelves, but it always felt cold and very oppressive. It was extremely difficult to fall asleep in there and you always felt like you were being watched. At night, I used to sleep with the bedside lamp on but would be conscious of something or someone staring at me from the very end of the room, nearest one of the windows. I would lay there awake for what seemed like an eternity and eventually fall asleep through exhaustion. I could never work out why I was so awake and unable to get comfortable enough to sleep.

It seemed my sister also felt this way although, at the time, we didn't discuss this. When she would stay at the house without me, she slept in that very room and years later eventually told me that she also struggled to sleep in there. However, she had an experience in that room that really scared her and set something in motion that changed my life and future forever.

One night, Serena was lying on one side of the bed, facing the wall, and felt something sit on the bed next to her. She assumed it was our younger sister, Lucy, as she often came in the room at night when we stayed over. Serena heard muffled crying and turned to check if Lucy was okay but saw a different girl sitting with her back towards her. Serena immediately noticed that it was not our younger sister. Her hair was different and she was dark but transparent. Serena knew instinctively it wasn't her and terror shot through her entire body. She screamed and yanked the bed covers to pull them over her head. The young girl vanished and the room instantly became icy cold.

Our father heard her screams and burst into the room. He immediately felt the cold and asked what had happened. Serena explained what she had just seen and expected a response of disbelief and logical reasoning, but instead he told her to calm down and just said, "Don't say anything to your sisters. I don't want them scared". It was like he knew what she had seen and perhaps was fully aware that the house was haunted!

Several years passed and we spent less time at their house. I went off to university in the north of England and my sister followed two years later, residing in Portsmouth on England's South Coast. It was the year 2000 and I was in my last year at university. I was living in a large, eight-bedroomed Victorian house with six other students. My bedroom was on the ground floor, situated in what would have been a drawing or dining room. Although the house was big and cold, it was comfortable and always busy. One night, I finished watching a movie upstairs in my flatmate's room and decided to head to bed. It was around 2am and I was quite tired. I turned out the bedroom light and got into bed, placing my mobile phone beside me. As always, I turned on my right side and faced the bedroom door. The room was dark, but light from the hallway was shining through beneath the door and I could still see the room and hear the others moving around in their rooms above me.

I had only closed my eyes for seconds when I felt someone grab my left arm and shake me, as if to get my attention. I remember thinking it was one of my friends and immediately shouted, "What do you want?" As soon as I opened my eyes the shaking sensation stopped, and I could see a young girl, aged about seven or eight, standing right by my bedside staring at me.

She appeared to be smiling and I could see her hair colour, skin colour, clothing and even the expression on her face, despite the room being dark. Within a second, a wave of fear came over me as I realised I could see through her too. She appeared to be made of light and I knew she was a spirit. I literally jumped backwards on my bed towards the wall and kicked a leg out to get away. I remember yelling as I did this, and watched her slowly dissipate and dissolve into the darkness of the room

I sat rigid with fear for a few seconds, scanning the area in disbelief. I knew what I had seen and thought, "I need to get out of here, now!" I was literally terrified and plucked up the courage to launch myself off the bed and run out of my room, leaving my phone still by my bedside.

I took off upstairs and ran into my friend Mark's room. I jumped into bed with him and told him that I had just seen a ghost in my room. He told me I was dreaming and laughed. I went and made a bed on the floor and tried to forget what happened.

The next morning, I forced Mark to come with me to retrieve my mobile phone and check my room. Everything was exactly the way I had left it the night before, but I still felt scared and spent the next few nights upstairs with my friends.

Skipping forward almost a year, I hadn't seen the ghost again and put it out of my mind a little. I graduated with honours and went back to live with my mother and stepfather in West London. I secured a job with a local TV company and met my wife, also named Lucy. We spent all our time together and she moved in with me at my parents' house. My sister Serena was in her first year of university over one hundred miles away and I hadn't seen her for months. One weekend Lucy and I decided to pay her a visit, so we drove down and surprised her. She was living in a basement apartment with one other flatmate. The flat was nice and had this long corridor leading into the kitchen. My sister's bedroom was located just before the kitchen and her flatmate Lizzie was next to her, nearest the lounge.

We enjoyed the evening and popped out for drinks and

dinner. That evening, the subject turned to ghosts, for some bizarre reason. My sister told us that they have a ghost in the apartment. I was curious and asked her more. She explained that they both often see a small child-like figure moving through the glass door of the kitchen from the corridor and Lizzie then told me an experience which she had not long ago. She said she went to bed and suddenly felt someone shaking her awake. As she opened her eyes, she saw a small girl standing in her room. I literally freaked and said, "No way … that's impossible!" I then told them all what I had encountered the year before. It was almost exactly the same experience and it blew my mind. How was this possible? I didn't know Lizzie, and my university was located almost three hundred miles from theirs.

That night, Lucy and I made a camp bed in the hallway, just outside my sister's bedroom. However, it wasn't long before Lucy became too scared and said, "I can't sleep out here." We decided to move into my sister's room but, due to lack of space, all three of us had to share her double bed. I went to close the door of the bedroom, but my sister said, "It's pointless, every time I close it, I wake up and it's open again." I thought, "That's new … and a bit a spooky." So, to test her assertion, I closed it and placed two pairs of our shoes against the door.

We all talked for a little and eventually fell asleep. At some point, during the early hours of the morning, I woke up to the familiar sensation of being shaken. I opened my eyes and quickly grabbed the bed to stop myself falling out. I reached out with one hand to wake Lucy and my sister, but they were seemingly awake and had actually witnessed the shaking incident for themselves. I jumped up and couldn't see the little girl in the room, but the bedroom door was partially open and the shoes had been pushed aside. My sister and Lucy both denied opening the door and we all stayed awake, puzzled as to what just happened. I felt less scared this time and more curious. I was determined to find answers to what we experienced and figure it all out.

A few months later and back home in London, Lucy and I were both asleep in bed, when both of us woke up around 3am for no apparent reason. We were facing each other and wide awake. I asked what was wrong and she said, "Nothing", but asked me the same thing. I thought, "That's a bit odd; why are we both suddenly awake at the same time in the middle of the night for no good reason?" I told her to go back to sleep and leant over to kiss her goodnight when we both heard a young girl say "Goodnight" to us. The voice came from between our heads, as if she were lying in the bed with us. We both stared at each other petrified for a few moments. The voice was so loud and clear and we were convinced there was a child in the room with us. I then jumped out of bed and searched under the bed, in the wardrobe and even out in the hallway. The house was silent and there was nobody up and about.

That was the last time either of us heard or saw the girl. Who was she? Was it the same child I saw years before at university? I spent the next few years considering many options and the whole bizarre experience led me on a path of personal and spiritual discovery. It was that whole experience that pushed me to seek answers to the paranormal and ultimately led to me developing my own paranormal society.

It now seems plausible to me that this little girl was the same spirit that myself and my sister had first encountered several years before at our father's house. She had followed me and then my sister and wanted to show herself to us. I regret never asking her who she was or her name. To this day, I think about her a lot and wonder if she wanted to tell me something important. There is always a reason behind all experiences and this one seems to be connected to me and my sister. Perhaps one day she'll make herself known to me again and hopefully I'll be ready to help her and answer the many questions that I have mulled over for almost the last twenty years.

MORE FROM ERICA

Ghosts, Demons and Dolls True Ghost Stories & Hauntings Book 1): getBook.at/GDandD

Angels, Ghosts and Demons (True Ghost Stories & Hauntings Book 2): getBook.at/AGandD

Contact Erica: gammonsghosts@gmail.com

Printed in Poland
by Amazon Fulfillment
Poland Sp. z o.o., Wrocław